UNIVERSITY OF CALIFORNIA
PUBLICATIONS IN HISTORY

VOLUME XXXVII
1949

EDITORS

L. K. KOONTZ
D. K. BJORK
J. W. CAUGHEY
C. N. HOWARD

A PROSPECT OF CODRINGTON COLLEGE

"A, the College 210 feet in length. B, Mansion House. C, Windmill. D, Boiling House. E, Curing House. F, Consets Bay."

From William Mayo's *A New & Exact Map of the Island of Barbados in America According to An Actual & Accurate Survey* published in London in 1722.

CODRINGTON CHRONICLE

An Experiment in Anglican Altruism on a
Barbados Plantation, 1710-1834

EDITED BY
FRANK J. KLINGBERG

UNIVERSITY OF CALIFORNIA PRESS
BERKELEY AND LOS ANGELES
1949

University of California Publications in History

Editors (Los Angeles) : L. K. Koontz, D. K. Bjork, J. W. Caughey,
C. N. Howard

Volume 37, pp. x + 1–157, frontispiece

Submitted by editors August 15, 1947
Issued April 15, 1949
Price, cloth, $3.00 ; paper, $2.00

University of California Press
Berkeley and Los Angeles
California

◇

Cambridge University Press
London, England

PRINTED IN THE UNITED STATES OF AMERICA

PREFACE

FOR A two-year period during the war a seminar group met in Room L-48 of the Library, University of California, Los Angeles, on Thursday evenings and worked as a unit on the Codrington plantations documents. After ten years of borrowing manuscripts from the Library of Congress, a microfilm of the complete holdings of the manuscripts of the Society for the Propagation of the Gospel in Foreign Parts, of the Lambeth and Fulham Palace collections, and of the Thomas Bray Associates collection was obtained. On the arrival in Los Angeles of these films, purchased for use at the University of California Library, Los Angeles, a survey of the Codrington plantations in Barbados was undertaken.

The research for such a study was undertaken by nine persons and, ultimately, six investigations were completed. In preparation for the seminar meetings each worker sat in front of a film-reading machine and searched the illuminated page for his characters: the manager of the plantations, the schoolmaster, the foreman of the sugar house, the slaves, the agent in Bridgetown, and the Bishop of London, an ex-officio slaveholder. All the investigators contributed to the sum of the findings, and each of those able to continue to the end has his name on a chapter. Three of the group are now members of the departments of history at the University of Texas, at Rutgers University, and at the California Institute of Technology. Two others whose work is embodied in the present study but who were called away by war exigencies must be remembered here: Mary Carter and Louis Goodman.

The S.P.G. Manuscripts dovetail into other eighteenth-century source collections. Their value has been emphasized by the late Charles M. Andrews as well as by other historical scholars, social scientists, and librarians. Studies closely related to that on the Codrington plantations were carried on concurrently on the Los Angeles campus. A few, of thesis length, may be mentioned. Doctoral dissertations deposited in the Library of the University of California, Los Angeles, are: Robert Worthington Smith, "The Conflict between Planter and Parliament over the Slave Laws of Jamaica"; Samuel Clyde McCulloch, "The Life and Times of Dr.

Thomas Bray (1656–1730), A Study in Humanitarianism"; John Duffy, "A History of Epidemics in the American Colonies"; Maud E. O'Neil, "Samuel Andrew Peters, Connecticut Loyalist"; and J. Harry Bennett, "The Slaves on Society and College Plantations, Barbados, 1710–1834"; and a Master's thesis: "Early American Schoolbooks and Libraries as Revealed in the Records of Thomas Bray and the Society for the Propagation of the Gospel in Foreign Parts," by Helen E. Livingston. Other shorter works, using the same materials, and prepared at the same time, are cited in the notes at the end of this volume.

Acknowledgments are due for generous grants to the American Philosophical Society, the Phelps-Stokes Foundation, and the Church Historical Society, organizations whose support, like that of the universities, is basic to investigations requiring a period of years to develop. Thanks are due to President Robert Gordon Sproul and to the Board of Research of the University of California for hearty support for many years, to its Librarian for the purchase of the film and necessary equipment with which to use it, and to Dr. St. George L. Sioussat, Chief of the Manuscript Division of the Library of Congress, for the filming of so vast a manuscript collection. Upon this microfilming all the research depended. The Huntington Library arranged the filming of the Annual Sermons and the Abstracts of Proceedings and gave constant assistance from its research staff. The late William Webb Kemp, Dean of the School of Education at Berkeley for many years, gave to the project his collection of notes taken during a long residence in England. This material proved of particular value for the educational aspects of the Codrington plantations study.

The index was prepared by Ruth M. Winton.

Citations to the manuscript collections have been made to correspond with their arrangement in the microfilm materials as used at the University of California, Los Angeles. This arrangement usually corresponds to their archival arrangement in the Manuscript Division of the Library of Congress. In the case of the Miscellaneous Unbound Documents it varies somewhat, but all citations can easily be identified at either repository. To aid in this identification, the following abbreviations have been used throughout the notes: (L.C. Trans.) for the Library of Congress Transcripts; (L.C. Photo.) for the Library of Congress photographic reproductions; and for the Miscellaneous Unbound Documents (L.C. film), to designate the Library of Congress master film, rather than the Manuscript Division's archival arrangement of enlargements made from the master film.

Not all spelling, capitalization, and punctuation practices of the original documents have been preserved; all superior letters have been eliminated. With respect to chronology before 1752 the month and day are retained as given, but the year is made New Style.

FRANK J. KLINGBERG

University of California, Los Angeles

CONTENTS

INTRODUCTION

By FRANK J. KLINGBERG

INTRODUCTION

THE STORY of Codrington plantations is that of a conflict between two worlds. In the complex society of eighteenth-century England, wealth was so distributed that great variety of opinion flourished: the rich manufacturer could criticize the landlord; the East Indian merchant could quarrel with the West Indian; the woolen or linen business could point out the iniquity of the cotton trade; established wealth could scorn the new. In general, the reformer had a program for the other man's business. These disputes were carried on publicly in Parliament and between pamphleteers engaged on one side or the other. The Anglican Church itself faced vested interests and endured such threats as Walpole's hint to Bishop Edmund Gibson of disestablishment in the event of excessive reformatory zeal in London.

Overseas, in the islands of the West Indies, the planter struggled to produce wealth from his crops in an economically simple society. The crop was sugar, its by-products rum and molasses. The labor was slave, seasoned or fresh from Africa. The owner of a sugar plantation, often an absentee landlord in Britain, and the manager on the spot had one objective: to produce a money crop. They confined their thinking to the market, to the price of slaves and of sugar, and to the disasters of the season. Competition was keen between planters on an island, between one English island and another, and between English islands and those belonging to foreign powers. The usual correspondence between the Old and the New World was that of business. The annual ledger tied Britain to the island world.

The normal routine of making a fortune and taking it out of the islands was broken in 1710 when Christopher Codrington, a man who knew both worlds, divided his fortune between them. He had fought in the European wars, also in the campaigns in the islands. On the occasion of his attack on the French island of Guadeloupe (1703), he made his will, bequeathing his West Indian plantations to the Society for the Propagation of the Gospel to "maintain a convenient Number of Professors and Scholars" on the estates from the proceeds of the sugar. His provisions to the legacy were subject to various interpretations. The Barbadians wished to use the funds

for the education of white residents. But Bishop William Fleetwood, in England, at once viewed the gift as a foundation for
Negro Christianization and education.

Inspired by the legacy, Fleetwood in 1711 preached the Society's
Annual Sermon in which are to be found the later arguments
for the emancipation of the Negro. The strong words that the
Negroes "were equally the Workmanship of God with themselves
[the planters] ; endowed with the same faculties and intellectual
powers; Bodies of the same Flesh and Blood, and Souls certainly
immortal," made this sermon the charter of liberties for the Negro
race and the choice for wide distribution throughout the eighteenth
century; indeed it is of interest even today as a technique in the
reform and the eventual abolition of an entrenched institution. At
one time two thousand copies of the sermon were sent to the West
Indies at the request of the S.P.G. missionaries.

Concerning the slaves on the Codrington estates, the Bishop declared, "that if all the Slaves throughout America, and every
Island in those Seas, were to continue Infidels for ever, *yet ours
alone must needs be Christians.* We must instruct them in the
Faith of Christ, bring them to Baptism, and put them in the way
that leads to everlasting Life. This will be preaching by *Example*,
the most effectual way of recommending Doctrines, to a hard and
unbelieving World, blinded by Interest, and other Prepossessions."
In this early sermon, Fleetwood encompassed all that would follow
and was, in that sense, the discoverer of the black race and the
prophet of its future Christianization and education in Anglo-
Saxon America.[1]

Thus by means of the Codrington gift the two worlds, old and
new, met within one corporation. To the Society, the Negro was a
man with a soul. To the planter, he was a chattel, a piece of property, a tool. The Society, however, now owned this tool on the
Codrington plantations, and through the course of a century and
a quarter, proceeded on its assumption that in a humane regime
the Negro could become a Christian, educated and skilled, and yet
remain, by the law of the Colony, in a state of slavery.

This concept may seem less than a revolution to the twentieth-
century mind, but in 1710 it was radical to an extreme degree. The

---

[1] For notes to the Introduction, see p. 125.

Society's Negroes were to become Christian slaves. To slaveowners this program was the first step to freedom. Once the Negro was granted a soul, his freedom would follow. In this conviction, the slaveowner was right. Instructions from the Society that slavery was not to be interfered with, opinions of the solicitor general and the attorney general in England that Christianity was not emancipation, learned arguments that the Christian slave who could read and write would be a better slave, did not ease the planter's fears that his property would become free. The logic of events moved slowly but directly to that end.

The story of Codrington plantations is not that of a Utopia, but a thoroughly documented chapter from the life of the eighteenth century. Both in England where the Society had its center, and on the island where the experiment was under hostile observation, the enterprise was conducted in the atmosphere of hereditary property rights, rigid legal limitations, and the controlling conceptions of a mercantilist empire. The Anglican Church itself operated in this framework from which it could not escape nor make far-reaching alterations in the economic society of Britain.

In England and in the Empire, reforms were a modification upon the body politic, wherein institutions were changed by pressures coming from within this existing society. For example, in his day Christopher Codrington could not have emancipated his slaves, thereby destroying his property, nor could the S.P.G., according to the terms of the will itself have introduced such a radical revolution. The reformer of that time could succeed by tying his cause to a respected and stable institution. The Church, representing the religious faith of the country, and cautious in its ideas, was a power and a force of remarkable tenacity. In this instance, the ideal that all men had souls could be put into practice by the men of the Church who, organized in London, were sufficiently remote from the sugar kettle to be largely indifferent to the hostility of the local planters. The Society, moreover, could finance its program during periods of hard times in sugar production, by drawing on its general funds, and at the same time it could steadily recruit its personnel.

The disasters of the slave economy in Barbados were such that, except for this support, financial bankruptcy and a depleted staff would, otherwise, have closed Codrington early in its history. At first sight, the Codrington experiment on 800 acres with 300 slaves, may seem to be of limited interest, but it was, in fact, regarded by all parties from the beginning as an experiment station. It figured as a laboratory in the later crusade for the Christianization of native peoples in India, Australia, and elsewhere. The work of Francis Le Jau in South Carolina, of Elias Neau in New York, of the Charleston Negro school, and activities in other centers of experiment were constituent parts of the wide activity of the Society which must be studied as a whole and in its separate units.

Humanitarianism in the course of a century shifted from the acceptance of the view that the Negro could be a Christian and a slave to the more radical position that slavery was contrary to the Christian spirit and therefore that emancipation was necessary. The mood or *Zeitgeist* of the thinkers before the beginning of the French Revolution included the theory of "the noble savage" and a current flowing not only from Christian thought but also from deistic sources. Transformation of opinion in England, a subtle and gradual change, was all to the benefit of such experiments as Codrington. The Negro came to be regarded as a white man enslaved, and therefore all the motives which would arouse men to set their brothers free came into operation. The basic fact of antislavery drives was the idea that the Negro, free of his chains, would have the motives of the white man to produce for himself and for export, to save, to establish himself and his community on British models. Such expectancies were utterly foreign to the island planter.

How fortunate, then, that the program of humanitarianism was not dependent on the islander. With legality on his side and profits the goal, he was overcome only by the continuity and intensity of the organized forces working for amelioration, and then emancipation. Except for Zachary Macaulay and James Stephen, the leading antislavery men did not know the institution at first hand and were therefore free to give full reign to their own idealistic conceptions. The S.P.G. was informed by its practical efforts to operate a slave plantation and to make money to use for the improvement of the plantation schools and the Negro's well-being. The Society's profits were subject to the same laws of production as those of neighboring capitalists. But the Society managed Codrington plantations far from local Barbados opinion and prejudice, and firmness of objective came from long-distant management.

The Society as an instrument for reform was toughened by its universal experience in meeting with resistance on the ground of operation, wherever it was. The strategy of the S.P.G. appears in all of its undertakings and is embedded in the vast mass of its records. The very fact that these records have been preserved, to yield their day by day, month by month story of a sugar plantation for a century, is itself a commentary upon the undiscouraged zeal and the long-range point of view which characterized the Society from its beginnings. The long story of a valuable manuscript collection and its survival may be condensed into a short statement. The records of the Society for the Propagation of the Gospel in Foreign Parts, of Fulham and Lambeth Palace, and of the Thomas Bray Associates were gathered and preserved by the secretaries of the societies and by the officials of the Bishop of London and the Archbishop of Canterbury. These collections of material form one major source and, for a survey of the subject, should be regarded as a unit. They were explored by American scholars for their value in the study of our colonial period, notably by Charles M. Andrews and Frances G. Davenport, in their descriptively titled, *Guide to the Manuscript Material for the History of the United States to 1783. In the British Museum, in Minor London Archives, and in the Libraries of Oxford and Cambridge.* The collection for the Library of Congress was completed through the generosity of Mr. John D. Rockefeller, Jr.

These accounts form a most important source for an understanding of American character, the processes of Americanization, and the broad story of the growth of American culture. The S.P.G. founded not only Codrington College, but also Columbia University. Active in 202 Central Stations throughout British America between 1701 and 1785, the Society sent out 353 missionaries and numerous schoolteachers, medical men, and libraries. In many of the colonies the first schools and libraries were founded by its representatives, and the fact that the program included Indians and Negroes, as well as white colonists, made it a force in many communities. Many aspects of colonial life are illuminated. As a mine of information the documents are inexhaustible, forming a great body of nongovernmental materials.

The arguments for the study of American religious history were never more ably stated than by the late J. Franklin Jameson in his presidential address, "The American Acta Sanctorum," before the American Historical Association and published in the *American Historical Review* (January, 1908). The continual revision of emphasis in history should include new studies of Anglo-American society and its deep wells of private benevolence and humanitarianism. Men interested in history, Anglo-Colonial relations, political science, economics, sociology, Americanization, anthropology, medicine, health and disease, and foods, will find that the missionary has taken notes for him. There are observations on plant and animal life, and specific information on agriculture and business, prices and colonial currency, intercolonial communication, the transit of ideas, population growth, relations with Negroes and with Indians, and contact with Europeans—Frenchmen, Spaniards, Germans, Swiss, and French Huguenots, as well as new light on the Dutch and the Swedes. The exactness of this information cannot be overemphasized. To cite one example, in the colonies, selection of titles and particular editions of the books are specified. The colonial hunger for books is revealed, together with the techniques of securing the return of stolen books by an appeal to conscience.

In the realm of ideas, no movement in philosophy, such as deism, no conflict with Quakers or Calvinists, no friction with Anabaptists or Methodists, no "threat" from Roman Catholics, goes unnoted. The missionaries in the colonies were compelled to fill out and send to England two elaborate questionnaires each year, and were encouraged to write frequently about every conceivable question that might arise. They were constantly advised from London and asked to carry out definite policies as a group and as individuals. Often graduates of Oxford, Cambridge, Trinity College (Dublin), Edinburgh, and Glasgow, as well as of American colleges they, at times, reported with a skill worthy of a Swift, a Defoe, or a Fielding, sketching the colonial scene in unforgettable terms. Their task was to interpret colonial society and its customs to the people of England, and in doing that they furnished exact information on subjects of colonial interest for the student today.

From the English side of the Atlantic, the intricate web of contact of the Society in the homeland is most informative. The money for the colonial venture was largely collected in England and, therefore, summaries were compiled annually and, in the form of Abstracts of Proceedings, circulated in the 15,000 parishes and the dioceses of England and Wales. Customarily bound with the Abstract was the Annual Sermon, a report to the nation on the conditions in the colonial world. One of the greatest honors that could be paid an eighteenth-century clergyman was to be asked to give one of these sermons. Bishops Burnet, Berkeley, Butler, Warburton, and Shipley are a few of the men who give us an insight into the English mind and English opinion of the colonial world.

The bishops were amazingly direct. Pointing to the great profits made in trade, it was declared, in one instance, that £1,000 each would be a fit recompense to humanitarian projects for the success achieved in business by wealthy Londoners. Moreover, the supply of men was a responsibility of the Society as urgent as the supply of money. Thus, as the organization specifically charged with the task of building an Anglican civilized society, the S.P.G. was a notable influence in promoting a humanitarian culture in the colonies of North America from Newfoundland to Barbados. In its field, the Society was as important as was the East India Company, for instance, in founding a business empire in India.[2]

The long records of the plantation at Codrington, unmatched in the history of Negro slavery, first attracted attention to the subject of this study. The second factor in the selection was the extraordinary example of a humanitarian enterprise based on the profits from sugar, rum, and molasses produced by slave labor. The estates were overvalued by the Society in 1710, since the peak of sugar production in Barbados, from the standpoint of profits, had already passed. Toward the end of the century there was a revival of prices brought about by the destruction of the rival French and other sugar islands by Negro insurrection. But in 1710, after nearly one hundred years of cultivation, Barbados no longer had virgin soil, abundant in other West Indian islands, and scientific methods of farming did not evolve until the nineteenth century.[3]

The Society thus took over a difficult income property, a major factor in the many misadventures. A private owner might have abandoned the estates in bankruptcy, but under the eighteenth-century view of contracts, a legacy could not be readily dissolved. The Society, in any event, was resolved to carry out the terms of its trust which it did, indeed, with rigidity. The Society might have been a pioneer in an earlier emancipation, but instead it held its slaves until they were emancipated by Act of Parliament (1833–1834), despite the ridicule of Sir George Stephen who referred to the Society as the Honorable Bench of Bishops and Slaveholders, Incorporated. Yet the gift of General Codrington, in 1710, had set in motion a revolutionary idea. The S.P.G. enterprise on Codrington plantations was designed to make the Negro a Christian, all, it is true, while he remained a slave. Indeed, the expectancy was that he would be more valuable as a blacksmith, cooper, potter, skilled cook, spinner, weaver, or field hand.

Profits were to go to the owner, the S.P.G., to be used in the Christianization of Negroes. All this revolution was to take place upon a plantation in the heart of an island committed to sugar growing for profit. The attorneys who were the managers of Codrington were usually also the owners of other slave-worked plantations. The accusations that they were *saboteurs,* working against the Christianization of Negroes, and for the maintenance of a white school, persist through most of the one hundred and twenty-five years of the plantation's life.

The story, then, of the Codrington experiment is that of a missionary ideal attempting to penetrate a regime of slavery. The S.P.G. had to function in this world of capitalism, predatory tactics, international rivalry, and humanitarianism. The Society drew its funds from an England which rejoiced in a torchlight procession when the news arrived that the monopoly of the Spanish slave trade had been won at Utrecht in 1713. The slave empire, as a part of mercantilism, was on the whole profitable, yielding 24 per cent per annum to the shippers, but it was often a submarginal affair to the planters themselves, and death to the sailors.

One hundred years after the Peace of Utrecht, torchlight processions again formed, this time to celebrate the abolition of the trade. Slowly the homeland of Africa became a safer haven for its population. Slowly the western world saw the Negro increase by births over deaths. Today in the United States, the 14 million Negroes are Christians, a religious achievement of prodigious effort comparable to the whole missionary enterprise in Asia. Codrington plantations, founded in the swelling tides of the slave trade, when Africa stocked the Americas with a labor force, and supported by the official missionary society of the Anglican Church, is a milestone in the story of white and black relationship from 1710 to 1834, from the Peace of Utrecht to British emancipation of slaves.

The larger subject of which Codrington is a chapter is that of Atlantic migration from Europe and from Africa. Up to 1860, probably more Negroes made the direct crossing from Africa to the Americas than Europeans going west from their shores. The estimated number of Negroes who were uprooted from Africa by the slave trade and crossed the ocean is 15 million. In the western world they are 30 million in number today. They made tropical America a productive unit. Tobacco, cotton, sugar, indigo, rice, and rum and molasses were crops and products usually produced under a capitalistic plantation regime.

The earlier Pacific migration from Asia had peopled the Americas, including the West Indies, with Indians. Now their descendants, also some 30 million in number, are, in certain areas, the mass base of the population of Latin America. In the West Indies, however, the Indians were not suited to the economic regime and did not long survive the European conquests. The missionary societies were confronted at the same time in the Caribbean region with the opportunity of Christianizing both Indians and Negroes.

Organized Christianity was then, and indeed is still, the chief humanitarian force. The white immigrant to the West brought his religion with him and coöperated with men of like persuasions across the Atlantic. Communication, though slow in the eighteenth century, was handled in such an intelligent and effective way through travel and correspondence that men of good will acted as one body surmounting distances and national boundaries. Long periods of peace find men, as in Gladstone's time, more hopeful than in dark days when war has torn the fabric of peace, cut off ordinary communications in intellectual and cultural matters, and stifled trade and travel.

The history of the antislavery movement, in its literature more extensive, perhaps, than even Napoleonic material, establishes that link between men of diverse languages and cultures which has the greatest survival value: the link of humanitarian zeal. The humanitarian, whether because of his eccentric individuality or stern Christian principles, has in general stood by his banner. Of such men it may be said that their lives, their characters, and their principles do not shift as the times change. Their ideals and their achievements may be thought of as a unity. They do not "die" in one character and take up another before the tomb. Something prevents their "running with the hounds" against a cause dear to their vision of humanity.

Looking about over the field of casualties in history, we find here and there the man who has loved his fellow man of whatever origin and tradition and who has a vision that the world can be made more humane, more beautiful, more livable, and that the general welfare, the health and happiness of all of its inhabitants may be increased. Such as these were the men who founded the S.P.G. and who, through two and a half centuries, have worked for Christian brotherhood.

CHAPTER I

Of the Noble and Generous Benefaction of General Christopher Codrington; of the Society "composed of wise and good Men"; the unhappy Disputes with the late General's Executor; and the Society's concern to promote the good Design.

By Samuel Clyde McCulloch and
John A. Schutz

THE INTERPRETATIONS of the will of Christopher Codrington were of continual interest, for its terms were not clear on what property was included, on what claims against the property were allowable, and on what were the actual intentions of the donor. These complications, presented in Chapter I, arose from the usual legal controversies concerning slave property in law. The slave was both a chattel and a person: a subject presented in the monumental work of Helen Tunnicliff Catterall, *Judicial Cases Concerning American Slavery and the Negro*. The special value of this work lies in the fact that it is drawn directly from the court records of plantation areas in America and in the British possessions in the West Indies, covering the period when Negroes both free and slave were frequently involved in litigation. Especially interesting, in relation to the present study, are those cases concerning the rights of the Negro in acquiring skills and education under the slave regime.

OF THE NOBLE AND
GENEROUS BENEFACTION OF GENERAL
CHRISTOPHER CODRINGTON

ODRINGTON COLLEGE and plantations, owned and operated by the Society for the Propagation of the Gospel in Foreign Parts, and situated in one of the richest British possessions, the sugar island of Barbados, has a continuity of records perhaps unrivaled by any other colonial institution of its kind. Details of operation and management were faithfully recorded year by year in the London office of the Society.

Christopher Codrington, a wealthy sugar planter, had been so impressed with the purpose of the great Anglican missionary society that, in 1703, he willed three plantations and 300 Negro slaves to the care and management of the S.P.G. to further its missionary program.

In a sense, Codrington's bequest was a challenge, and as such it was accepted by the Society. From the pulpit and in their litera- ture the leaders of the S.P.G. had taken an unequivocal stand for the human rights of native peoples in the Colonies, and of slaves on English-owned plantations. It was one thing to believe that a Christian slave was a happier and a better slave and another thing to prove it. Since the medical and missionary work in Barbados was to be supported from the production of sugar on the planta- tions, the will specifically stated that 300 Negroes were to be kept on the estates. The Society thus found itself in the business of sugar production, and in the unenviable position of using a slave regime to Christianize and civilize its own Negroes as an example for other planters to follow.

When Christopher Codrington died, on April 7, 1710, he was one of the wealthiest sugar planters in the West Indies. Curiously, the writing of his will was as remarkable as its contents. It was a "Soldier's Will," written "in his boots when he was going to Com- mand the Expedition to Guadalupe."[1] The document made many liberal bequests besides the generous gift of slaves and sugar plan- tations to the Society for the Propagation of the Gospel. All Souls

---

[1] For notes to chap. i, see pp. 125–127.

[15]

College, Oxford, received his private library and £10,000. The money was to be utilized in the construction of a new library building at All Souls and for the purchase of additional books. William Codrington, his cousin, received most of the personal property, one-half of the island of Barbuda, and plantations on St. Christopher's and Antigua. Several distant relatives and a few friends were also remembered in the will by smaller grants of money and property.

The Society soon learned that, except for the bare details of the bequest which listed three extensive plantations and awarded them 300 slaves, few other facts were immediately available except the curious conditions of the will which specified Codrington's desires:

... to have the plantations continued Intire and three hundred negros at least Kept always thereon, and A Convenient number of Professors and Scholars Maintained there, *all of them to be under the vows of Poverty Chastity and obedience,* who shall be obliged to Studdy and Practice Physick and chyrurgery as well as divinity, that by the apparent usefulness of the former to all mankind, they may Both indear themselves to the People and have the better oppertunitys of doeing good to mens Souls whilst they are Takeing care of their Bodys. But the Particulars of the Constitution I leave to the Society Compos'd of good and wise men.[2]

Christopher Codrington was, indeed, no ordinary man. He was a graduate of Oxford, a student of the classics, a brave soldier, and a successful administrator. He was born in Barbados in 1668, the son of a colonial who had engaged in the smuggling trade with the French and had amassed one of the greatest fortunes in the West Indies. Christopher Codrington was in England in 1700, when Thomas Bray and his associates were laying plans for the formation of the S.P.G. Its enlightened objectives may have interested him then because he had just been appointed governor of the Leeward Islands and was preparing to return to the West Indies to assume his new duties. Codrington would seem to have been sensitive to the need for well-educated men in the Anglican Church. For he had lived in the West Indies as a boy and had gone from there to England's finest schools. He attended All Souls College and Christ Church, Oxford, and spent many months studying law at the Middle Temple. At Oxford he was acclaimed as a poet, and

some of his contemporaries elevated him to the ranks of an author
of distinction. A few lines will show the quality of his art:

> Ask me not, friend, what I approve or blame,
> Perhaps I know not why I like or damn;
> I can be pleased and I dare own I am.
> I read thee over with a lover's eye,
> Thou hast no faults or I no faults can spy,
> Thou art all beauty or all blindness I.[3]

During his lifetime he was well-known as a book collector. In
1706 his library numbered 12,000 books and was valued at £6,000.
He hoped to make it the equal of any private library in Europe.[4]
Although he distinguished himself as an officer in the armies of
William III and Queen Anne, he is better remembered as governor
of the Leeward Islands.[5] During his relatively short term of three
years as governor, he was able to prosecute several vigorous as-
saults against the French, and in domestic affairs he sponsored
measures intended to reconstruct the judicial system and reform
the tax structure. As an executive, Codrington was popular. As a
member of the local landed aristocracy, he championed the interests of the Colonies and pointed out the defects in colonial administration, which provoked tension between the local and home
governments.

The unusual energy with which he executed the tasks of his gov-
ernorship wore down his health until he had to apply for a leave
of absence. But, instead, the Board of Trade removed him from
office. For the seven remaining years of his life, he journeyed in
the West Indies, looking after his many properties, fighting the
encroachments of royal authorities, and seeking to recover his
health.[6] Essentially, Christopher Codrington was a man of action.
But in his writings, and especially in the terms of his will, he
emerges as a man of ideas as well. Especially significant is the fact
that he wished to extend religious advantages to the colored peoples
of the Colonies.

Exactly 180 years after Codrington wrote his will, Sir John
Seeley, in contrasting life of emigrants in the North American
settlements with the comparative luxury of West Indian plantation life, arrived at a similar conclusion. In 1883, Seeley drew
a sharp line between the ultimate success of the American conti-

nental colonies and the decline of the West Indian plantations. The religious emigrants to North America had brought with them the tools of culture, religion, and settlement. But in the West Indian world, as in Asia and Africa, the founders "carried no Gods with them," going instead into "the wilderness of mere materialism." In Seeley's words, an emigrant "who goes out merely to make his fortune may in time forget his native land; but he is not likely to do so; absence endears it to him, distance idealizes it; he desires to return to it with his money...." Religion, as a civilizing and stabilizing influence, Seeley concluded, "makes all the difference."[7]

As a native West Indian, Codrington understood that educational institutions in the Colonies would not only reduce traveling expenses for young men of ambition, but tap new reservoirs of man power and help build a more complete society. Properly staffed and well equipped, these institutions could bring specialized training to colonials to meet the problems of their environment. Well educated, the natural leaders of the community would acquire sound religious principles and a respect for English culture and learning. More important, the Colonies would not be denuded of their able young men who, after being educated in England, either stayed there or went to other parts of the Empire.

Why, it may be asked, did Christopher Codrington choose the S.P.G. as his beneficiary and the trustee of his college? When he made his will, he must have been impressed by the vitality of the Society's program during the first years of its organization. The able builders of the Society had adopted a program and at once carried it into action. The London office functioned with the efficiency of a great profit-making corporation, and Codrington must have believed it could be entrusted with the management of the Barbados plantations. The S.P.G. sprang from the widespread desire of many religious Englishmen at the end of the seventeenth century to stimulate, within the community, a higher Christian morality. In its famous organizer, Thomas Bray, were blended the abilities to conceive an idea, to present it orally and in writing, and to bring measures to a successful conclusion through the assistance of the greatest men of his age.[8]

On June 27, 1701, the Society met for the first time. Clerics and laymen of distinction attended the meeting. They included, among others, the Archbishop of Canterbury, Thomas Tenison, who added great dignity to the occasion by presiding over the assembly; the Bishops of London (Henry Compton), Bangor (John Evans), and Gloucester (Edward Fowler); Sir John Philips; Sir George Wheler; Dr. Gideon Harvey, a doctor of medicine and nephew of the famous William Harvey; the Dean of St. Paul's (Thomas Sherlock); and White Kennett, the Archdeacon of Huntingdon.[9] After prayer the Archbishop of Canterbury opened the assembly. The charter was read, officers were elected, and committees appointed.[10]

The preamble of the S.P.G. charter set forth the threefold objects of the Society. It proposed, first, the maintenance of an orthodox clergy in the plantations, colonies, and factories of Great Britain beyond the seas. Second, it promised to furnish all provisions necessary for the propagation of the gospel in those parts. Finally, it planned the management and disposition of funds to be raised for the missionary program by the solicitation of the charity of his Majesty's subjects. In the first anniversary sermon of the Society the Dean of Lincoln, Richard Willis, elaborated on these provisions of the charter:

The design is . . . to settle the state of religion, as well as may be among our own people there, which, by all accounts we have, very much wants their pious care, and then to proceed in the best methods they can towards the conversion of the natives: both these are works that will require a great expense—the sending ministers thither, and maintaining them in many places where they have no settled maintainance; the procuring libraries to encourage ministers to go thither, and to enable them to do their duty the better when they are there; the breeding up of persons to understand the great variety of languages of those countries, in order to be able to converse with the natives, and preach the Gospel to them.[11]

From the first, the Society recognized that a vital part of its work must be a program for Negroes, especially for slaves in the plantation colonies.[12] Indeed, the strong stand for the Christianization of Negroes made by the Society in these early years, may well have been the decisive factor in Christopher Codrington's choice of the Society as the trustee for his estates. Two years before the S.P.G. was founded he had written regarding the state of the slaves in the plantations, had urged their right to be Christians, and had added, ". . . 'tis certain the Christening of our Negroes without the instructing of them would be useless to themselves and pernicious to their masters."[13]

One of the most important decisions during the early years of the Society was that of choosing an outstanding churchman each year to preach an Annual Sermon before the assembled members on the third Friday in every February. Frank J. Klingberg, in *Anglican Humanitarianism in Colonial New York,* has noted the importance of these sermons:

> From the very foundation of the S.P.G., the annual sermon was an outstanding ecclesiastical event.... Like the Government's speech from the throne on the state of the nation, the sermon was a survey of the state of the church at home and abroad; it drew the attention of all men to the missionary engaged in distant fields, in contact on the frontier with native peoples and with the puzzling problems of empire expansion....[14]

Likewise important to the young organization was the program for raising money to finance these enterprises. At the second meeting the Archbishop of Canterbury generously agreed to pay for the printing of 5,000 copies of the Charter.[15] His support was again apparent at the next meeting when his was far the largest donation.[16] Not until 1704 did the S.P.G. publish its first account. The little booklet was divided into three sections: what the Society had already done, what it planned to do, and what encouragements it hoped for to enable it to continue.[17] Of the last named, money was the main consideration. On October 17, 1701, a form of subscription was decided upon which presently netted £184, and immediately afterwards subscription rolls were circulated throughout England; by the end of the year £204[18] had been gathered in. This type of fund gathering was carried on yearly, bringing in £500 to £950 in the early years. Private benefactors made frequent donations which far exceeded the subscriptions, and constituted a second method of financial support. From 1712 to 1834 the annual totals ranged from £2,060 to £68,437. These figures do not include the income of the Codrington trust.[19]

The money thus collected was immediately utilized. Missionaries were provided for the Colonies, churches and church organizations were set up, libraries were furnished to each missionary, the distribution of Church literature was provided for and, last, parish schools and colleges were established to train clergymen and teachers.

From the very outset the S.P.G. was painstaking in the training of its missionaries.[20] Each candidate was required to furnish such particulars as "age, condition of life, whether single or married, temper, prudence, sober and pious conversation, zeal for the Christian religion and diligence in his Holy Calling, affection for the present Government, and conformity to the doctrine and discipline of the Church of England."[21] His education and preaching ability were evaluated and, if he was not a native Englishman, his ability to pronounce the language correctly was considered.[22]

As soon as the letters of recommendation were passed upon, the lay candidate was ordained a deacon. According to canon law an aspirant to the deaconship had to be twenty-three years of age, or he must secure a dispensation from the Archbishop of Canterbury.[23] In order to qualify he must be examined by a bishop to determine his intellectual fitness, and test his knowledge of Greek, Latin, Scriptural and Church history, the Bible, Prayer Book, the Creeds, and the Thirty-nine Articles. He could also, if he wished, be examined in Hebrew.[24]

By the close of Anne's reign, in 1714, the Society was large and flourishing. An indication of the Society's prosperity appears in the analysis of the Abstract of Proceedings published with the Annual Sermon in 1713. Although it cited difficulties and delays encountered in "the good work," the "changeable affections of men" and the forces of prejudice,[25] and lamented that more missionaries were not being sent out, it concluded with an impressive list of legacies, gifts, and benefactions which the S.P.G. had received during the year, and listed the many new members. The final section included a record of the Queen's "Bounty and Goodness," a report on the prospective college at Codrington, and an auditor's statement.[26]

These Abstracts of Proceedings, which were published yearly with the Annual Sermon, provide a picture of the magnitude of the Society's work. At the center, in London, sat the executive body, sending orders, paying salaries, and receiving reports from all its missionaries in America and in the West Indies. These reports were made more systematic and effective by the requirement that each missionary keep a parish record, called the *Notitia Parochialis.*[27] In it he kept the names of his parishioners, the names of any who had made a profession of faith, lists of baptisms, communicants, and finally a summation of the principal difficulties which confronted him in his work. The contents of this report, therefore, provided the missionary with the bulk of the letter which he was required to send to London.

The Secretary of the S.P.G. brought these letters before the Society at the next meeting. A problem requiring special attention was delegated to a committee, or grouped with similar problems and considered as soon as possible. Nothing escaped the careful attention of the London body, the headquarters and clearing house of the whole vast program. The measure of its success appears in the Annual Sermon preached by Bishop Thomas Secker, afterwards Archbishop of Canterbury, who reviewed the Society's work in 1741:

> In less than forty years, under many Discouragements, and with an income very disproportionate to the Vastness of the Undertaking, a great deal hath been done; though little notice may have been taken of it, by Persons unattentive to these things, or backward to acknowledge them. Near a Hundred Churches have been built; above ten thousand Bibles and Common-Prayers, above a hundred thousand other pious Tracts distributed: great Multitudes, upon the whole, of Negroes and Indians brought over to the Christian Faith: many numerous Congregations have been set up, which now support the Worship of God at their own Expense, where it was not known before; and Seventy Persons are constantly employed, at the Expense of the Society, in the farther service of the Gospel.[28]

To understand the Society's administration of the Codrington estate it is, therefore, necessary to realize that the plantations in Barbados were but a part of a large program, which may account for some of the delays in communication and decision which sometimes seemed inexplicable to the men on the scene in Barbados.

Shortly after Christopher Codrington's death, on April 7, 1710, the Society was notified of his bequest. Because of its unusual provisions, a separate committee was appointed to consider his wishes and to carry them out. Attorneys were appointed for the care of the Society's affairs in Barbados. These men were instructed to request Colonel William Codrington, executor of the estate, to probate the will in order that the Society might be put into possession of the inheritance. Complying with their instructions the men visited William Codrington. He accepted the Society's right to the land and 300 Negroes, but maintained that the movables belonged to him.[29] He claimed all equipment, the cattle, the produce of all the cane growing at the time of Christopher Codrington's death, and the Negroes, in excess of the 300 slaves specified for the Society. Further, whatever debts or liens there were on the property belonged, not to him, but to the Society. As for Barbuda, Colonel Codrington took direct issue with the will. By its provisions, half of the Barbuda property was his. Since he and his cousin had held the entire Barbuda estate in joint tenancy as heirs of their fathers (John and Christopher Codrington, Sr.), William Codrington maintained that half of the three-eighths assigned to the Society was in reality his, and that the S.P.G. was entitled to only three-sixteenths of the island.[30]

The London officers of the Society, busy with plans to collect the proceeds from the plantations and to build a college, found this report something of a surprise.[31] Already plans for the college buildings were in preparation, and a separate Codrington fund had been established for handling the income from the estates.[32] Dudley Woodbridge and Gilbert Ramsay, the Barbados attorneys, again called upon William Codrington on February 1, 1712.[33] In the meantime, at the instigation of Governor Robert Lowther, they had brought suit in the Chancery Court of Barbados for possession of the estates. Codrington had demurred to the bill, leaving both sides in fear of a long litigation fatal to the property. The fear was heightened by suspicion of the Governor, the political enemy of Woodbridge and Codrington. Both men, therefore, were inclined to make a settlement to free themselves from litigation and Governor Lowther's intervention. At this moment proposed articles of agreement, satisfactory to the Society and to Codrington's agents in London, arrived in Barbados and were confirmed by William Codrington on February 2, 1712.[34]

By the terms of the agreement the Society was given immediate possession of the Barbados estates. It was permitted to keep all the Negroes and movable property. Debts and salaries outstanding before Christopher Codrington's death, and an annuity due Alexander Cunningham were matters not settled until 1742, when the Society received £5,000 from the heirs of William Codrington. It is also interesting that the final legal transfer of the Codrington family's claim to the two Barbados plantations was not made until 1742.[35] In that year the Society sought an agreement with Codrington on their respective claims in Barbuda. The Society, however, was not to profit from its Barbuda claim.[36]

Meanwhile, the Society had turned its attention to the greater task of fulfilling the wishes of the testator, and here again the will contained a problem. Christopher Codrington had provided for the construction and maintenance of a seminary in which medical missionaries were to be educated. Montagu Burrows, in his book the *Worthies of All Souls,* suggested that the Archbishop of Canterbury deleted from the will the phrase calling for monastic vows.[37] At any rate, the Society decided to found a college, not a monastic seminary, but with the primary purpose of training missionaries for the colonial field.

The combination of many circumstances, however, produced a classical grammar school of the English type. Indeed, it was not until 1745 that the physical and economic problems of building construction and the legal problems of settling the disputes with William Codrington and his heirs permitted even this institution to be opened. This school remained in operation until 1775, when it was closed until 1797. The second period of grammar school education may be said to extend to 1830, when the true college was opened. But the grammar school, to be known as the Lodge School, has continued to the present time.

Under the supervision of William Hart Coleridge, first Bishop of Barbados, the true college, equipped to educate men for the work of the Church in the West Indies was opened in 1830. Codrington College became and has remained the only college in the British West Indies and a chief source of supply for Church personnel.

CHAPTER II

Of the Buildings in Progress with which to House the College; of supplies wanting and the great Charge of building; of the Society's pleasure in the good work advancing in Barbados.

By MAUD E. O'NEIL

IN THE ACTUAL construction of the college there was little conflict of opinion. The expectancy that the task would be easily accomplished was not, however, fulfilled. Shortage of funds, of material, and of workers delayed construction for many years. An occasional hurricane blew down the fabric of the buildings. The importation from England of designs made by an eminent architect necessitated also importation of special materials and craftsmen to use them, thereby causing further delay. Long-distance management habitually defeats itself in grappling with local factors which might be handled successfully by native methods.

OF THE BUILDINGS IN PROGRESS WITH
WHICH TO HOUSE THE COLLEGE

CHRISTOPHER CODRINGTON had broadly sketched his plan of a school for training the youth of Barbados and medical missionaries, but it remained for the Society to develop it. Encouraged by early reports of prosperity on the plantations, the leaders of the Society assembled, almost as soon as they learned of the bequest, to lay plans for the college building. Undaunted by difficulties over the will, they decided to erect a few imposing buildings which would stand the shocks of tropical weather and endure like cathedrals of the past. Early in 1714 these arrangements were well under way, and the Annual Report announced:

The Society ... have resolved forthwith to begin the Building a College in *Barbadoes*, pursuant to the Directions and for the Purposes mentioned in the last Will of the General. There is a Model of the said College now preparing, by the kind Assistance and Direction of that worthy Gentleman, Colonel *Christian Lilly*, one of Her Majesty's Engineers, who formerly made a Present to the Society of a large Plan of their Estates in *Barbadoes*, which Model, when perfected will be sent over to *Barbadoes*. . . .[1]

Employed in 1713, Lilly worked for two years upon these very elaborate plans, with careful attention to every detail. The early plan, "humbly Dedicated to the Illustrious Society for the Propagation of the Gospel in Foreign Parts. By their Devoted Servant C. Lilly," was also published in the Annual Report.[2] The plan shows a large, rambling structure enclosing a quadrangle. The site of the college was between the two plantations on a particularly beautiful tableland rising about 200 feet above the level of the sea. This site was on the lower plantation with its chalky hills, and to the west toward Bridgetown was the upper plantation with a manse house, outlying buildings, three windmills, and slave quarters. The college building itself was to face south, or inland, with the white sandstone cliffs of St. John breaking the horizon in the immediate foreground. Waterfalls fell from the sheer sides of these cliffs to form a stream which flowed across the college campus, and turned east to water the plantation. Lilly's blueprints showed his appreciation of the scenic advantages of the site. The plans for the four units

---

[1] For notes to chap. ii, see pp. 127–129.

were labeled: that on the South side "Facing Towards a Rivulet, and to the Principal Avenue"; on the North side, "Facing toward pastures, etc., and Ocean about a Mile Distant"; on the East side, "Facing towards the Gardens and to the Ocean about 14 miles Distant"; and finally one for the West side "Facing towards the Old Buildings," which was "Term'd exactly like the East Side."[3]

Although specific consideration was given in the plan to the Barbados climate and the natural beauties of the site selected, the building was in some respects one that might have been more appropriately built in England than in Barbados. For, except for the stone for foundations and walls, the specified materials had to be shipped in at great expense. Bricks had to be sent from England on the slow sailing vessels; cedar, not indigenous to the country, had to be used for shingles; and certain types of finishing lumber, where native woods might well have been substituted, were required; and the heavy wrought iron for grills and casings had to come from across the seas.

The walls of the building were to be of stone six feet thick at the bottom, and reduced by offset to three feet at the top. Sir Robert Schomburgk, visiting the place a century later, commented upon the exceptional character of the walls which had withstood so many years of storm and tempest.[4]

Members of the Society had been contributing individually toward the enterprise which had caught their imagination and inflamed their zeal. This was, indeed, a common goal in which the scholar as well as the humblest citizen could contribute his share in building a school to train missionaries for carrying the Gospel to the New World. Early in the enterprise Mr. John Lane contributed a bell for the chapel.[5] In 1715, the Society announced that £50 had been received as the benefaction of Mrs. Margaret Matson and another £50 from Patrick Thompson, both citizens of Barbados. Through the Bishop of Norwich, "an Unknown Lady" in England contributed £100. Books were donated in England; £5 had been "lodged also upon the Spot in the Hands of Judge Woodbridge," expressly to buy books for the library.[6]

The following year brought additional gifts, chief of which was that of "his late Grace of Canterbury, who, whilst disabled and confined from public Business, by the Infirmities of Sickness and

old Age; was yet labouring in his Thoughts ... as appears from ...
the donation of a Library to Codrington."⁷ This Library consisted
of "the following proper and very valuable Books: viz. the *Poly-
glott Bible* of *London* in 6 Volumes Folio: the last Edition of
the *Book of Martyrs*, in 3 Volumes Folio; the *Summa of Thomas
Aquinas* in 1 Volume Folio; and Mr. *Ray* on *Plants* in 3 Volumes
Folio, Latin." Prominent citizens of Barbados had contributed
substantial sums: William Sharpe, Esq., £100 Sterling; William
Walker, Esq., £50 Sterling; and Paul Carrington, Esq., £20 Sterling "to the good work advancing in Barbados."⁸

Early in the proceedings the Society had decided to set up
commissioners and deputies chosen from the leading citizens of the
West Indies to "quicken *Benefactions* to the whole Building, Chappel, Library, Garden, Ornaments, &c." These men were also to serve
as sponsors for the school when it should be opened. The group
included usually the governors and prominent citizens not only of
Barbados but also of the Leeward Islands. The men were chosen to
secure community support for the founding of a college for the
whole West Indian world, which would "answer the longing Expectations of the worthy Gentlemen in those Parts, for the Benefit of
whose Posterity 'tis chiefly to be erected."⁹ A partial list of the Commissioners appointed in 1714 is typical:

... His Majesty's *Governour* or *Commander in Chief* of the Island of *Barba-
does*, for the Time being; the Honourable Colonel *William Codrington*, Colonel
Thomas Allen, Alexander Walker, Colonel *John Frere, John Colleton*, Colonel
Reynold Allen, Dudley Woodbridge, William Dotton, Colonel *Joseph Solimon*,
Colonel *Henry Peers*, Colonel *Edmund Durousseau, Edward Perry*, Esqrs;
the Reverend Mr. *Gilbert Ramsay*, Mr. *Charles Irwine*, Mr. *William Gordon*,
Clerks, and Mr. *John Lane*, Merchant: ... In the *Leeward Islands*, the *Gov-
ernour* or *Commander* in Chief for the Time being, his Excellency General
Walter Hamilton; in *Nevis*, the Reverend Mr. *Robert Robertson*, Colonel
Richard Abbot, Colonel *Daniel Smith, James Brown*, Esqrs; In *Antigua*, the
Reverend Mr. *James Field*, Colonel *Edward Byam*, Colonel *William Codrington*, Colonel *William Thomas*, Colonel *Thomas Williams;* in *St. Christopher's*,
the Reverend Mr. *Daniel Burchall, Ralph Willet*, Esq; *John Holden*, Esq;
George Liddal Wyse, Esq; *William Garrash*, Esq, *Daniel Raval*, Esq ... of
all whose Knowledge, Ability, Integrity and good Inclinations, the Society
have especiall Trust and Confidence.¹⁰

For four years the Annual Sermons had raised the hopes of the
Society's members that construction of the school would soon

begin. It was with considerable satisfaction, therefore, that they listened to Canon Thomas Hayley's sermon of February 15, 1717, which assured them that they were about to realize the promise. The account of progress in Barbados announced that the Society "are now come to a resolution to begin to lay the foundations without any further delay; having judged the fund they have in hand with what will annually arise from the estate . . . sufficient to support the great undertaking."[11]

Already the materials to begin construction, including several thousand bricks imported from England, were at hand.[12] A government man-of-war stationed at the island had been procured to bring necessary timber from the islands of Antigua and Tobago;[13] the plantation's wharf had been repaired to facilitate the landing of equipment; and the Society's order, that no more buildings were to be erected on the estates until the college was finished, was put into effect.[14] Committees were appointed and workmen were arranged for. The commissioners selected to supervise construction of the school were ordered to send detailed reports to the Society.[15] However, the immediate direction of the project was the task of John Smalridge, plantation manager.

The stone for the main part of the building was cut from the white limestone cliffs in front of the college site. It was soft and easy to handle, but when exposed to the air became hard, thus making an ideal material.[16] Lime also was available on the island, and consequently, during the early part of the construction there was no need to wait for materials coming long distances.

The most prominent retarding factor during this period, as later, was the labor problem. Because of the elaborate design of the buildings, especially skilled workmen had to be sent from England. These workmen were unaccustomed to the tropical climate, and, despite the care taken to provide suitable working conditions for them, they took sick and either succumbed, or, because of failing health, went back to England. One, William Gunyon, died before his assignment on the building was finished, and another, Joseph Cheltenham, stayed on after the death of Gunyon in spite of ill health, to complete his work on the elaborate cupola. Smalridge wrote about him to the Society, stating that Cheltenham had been paid the usual £40 for his services, that he was returning to London because of ill health, but that the manager hoped he might come back to Barbados, since he was a faithful and conscientious man.[17]

For common tasks of construction, Negroes from the plantation or hired men from other estates were employed. This labor, untrained and often unsatisfactory, was essential; for the stone had to be quarried from the cliffs, lifted to the wooden-wheeled oxcarts, and drawn over poorly constructed roads to the college site. Such work was slow and time consuming. In 1715 Dudley Woodbridge reported to the Society that the hired hands were still "chearfully" sawing stone.[18]

From time to time the attention and resources of the Society were drawn away from the building program of the college to meet the pressing business of sugar production. Cane must be hoed and cut, and boiling houses must be manned else there would be no sugar to market. Tropical storms made it necessary to harvest cane before it was flattened to the ground or washed entirely away; to hurry to shelter sugar on its way to market; to make fast equipment and buildings, and to secure stock against wind and rain.

A certain number of skilled workmen besides those sent out from England were essential to the building program. These men were difficult to obtain in Barbados, for the island was small and there was no supply of shifting, mobile labor. Those who lived on the island usually had their own places to look after, and hired help was unreliable. Many an item of a few day's payment here and there to a carpenter, smith, and painter is found on the books during these years. The following pay roll is typical.[19]

June 30, 1725   The Carver for carving 8 Capitals... £11
                The Smith for ironwork for the orna-
                   ment of the Cupola.............. £17.8s
                21 days work of a pair of Sawyers... £ 4.0.7½

Thus the problem of an adequate labor supply was one factor retarding the progress of the school.[20]

A somewhat drastic criticism of the building operations upon the plantation came from Charles Cunningham, rector of St. John's parish, who wrote the Society in 1717, just one year after the work on the buildings had been started. He stated that the agent for plantation affairs was receiving extravagant commissions running between £300 and £400 a year, that the stones inaccurately cut from the cliffs had to be recut after they had begun to harden, and thus it would cost the Society about £50,000 to build the college. Moreover, he charged that extensive building operations on the plantation itself were unnecessary. In spite of the more-than-adequate equipment on the upper plantation, the attorneys had, during the year just past, "built three . . . large houses upon it . . . a smith's and cooper's shop under one long roof, notwithstanding there is a very good cooper's and smith's shop in the lower plantation . . . and one cooper's shop above . . . so that now you have three cooper's shops . . . [and] another house two stories high . . . also a large house for a kitchen and buttery for the use of your negro driver. . . ."[21]

There is little doubt that the Society had visions far beyond its ability to pay, and that the wealth of the plantations had been greatly overestimated, especially in view of the lean years which began in 1718. Further, there was opportunity for handsome commissions to unscrupulous agents, because of the distance from England, and the lack of skilled labor also increased the cost of production. But a later investigation of Cunningham's statements revealed that many of them were exaggerations.

Because building operations went forward slowly during the first years, Barbadians were skeptical whether the college would ever be finished. However, one island planter felt that many of these criticisms against the school were unfair. After a visit to the Society's estates, he wrote a letter to a friend in England commending the work which was being done.

Sir, my curiosity prompted me the other day, to take a journey to Consetts, where I saw not only the foundation of the College laid, but a good part of it done: it will be the most beautiful, the most regular, and the noblest building we have seen on this side of the world; there seems to be a great deal of care and exactness, and the work is neatly and substantially done; the foundations of the main walls are six feet thick, and are reduced to three by proper offset, and are well banded with large stones; and are excellently good . . . Most of the principal timber is provided, and what I saw of it was very good, being the ground floors of the chambers which are laid; In a word I saw such prudent measures taken, and such preparations made, that I do not doubt I shall see the carcass of the building finished in a twelvemonth. You therefore cannot be insensible of the many vile aspersions which have been bruited abroad; and therefore you must imagine I was very agreeably deceived to find things in such a state, which made me resolve to be thus particular.[22]

Work on the masonry and main part of the college building dragged on for five years and was only finished in 1721. Since it had been the plan to support the project from the proceeds accruing from the estate, the construction could only progress when there were adequate profits. During the latter part of the period, crops had been poor and the sugar of an inferior quality, so that there was not money enough to carry on the work consistently. Materials could not be purchased promptly and advantageously, workmen could not be paid, debts had accumulated, and the outlook was generally discouraging.[23]

On March 2, 1722 the Society instructed its attorneys in detail on how to complete the college chapel.[24] The expenses in Barbados were so heavy that in 1721 the Society found it necessary to sell East India bonds to the value of £1,300.[25] With this help from the Society, the main part of the building was completed, the workmen, except certain skilled mechanics employed in the finishing work, were discharged, and the building commission disbanded.[26]

From this time on only the income from the estates was to be used to complete the interior of the college. Because of the crop failures during this period, with a subsequent reduction in profits, the amount that could be used annually was curtailed to £200.[27] This sum had to cover the expenses for both workmen and materials. Thus the finishing of the college was doomed to be long and tedious, unless by some future dispensation of Providence or by skillful management the plantation could produce optimum crops, adequate labor could be supplied, transportation difficulties removed, sugar markets remain good, and something of the former wealth of the estates could be realized. The main burden of this task rested squarely upon the shoulders of John Smalridge, plantation manager. Add to the already heavy load of plantation management the work of building a school elaborately planned by a group of idealists in England, and the additional obstacle of long-distance management, and the undertaking assumes heroic proportions.

The difficulty of long-distance management in the erection of Codrington College is sharply portrayed in Smalridge's correspondence with the Society. Details of the plans had to be changed from time to time to suit different conditions found in the island.

Four years after the building program had been begun, it was found necessary to substitute maselick wood for the chapel and hall window frames instead of the iron which had been sent from England for that purpose.[28] In April, 1724, eight years after the beginning of the project, Smalridge wrote the Society, "I have not seen any draft of the inside work of the chapel. Cedar ought to be prepared and laid by, as well as boards to season."[29] Three months later he wrote again rather plaintively, "I have never received any draft of the inside of the chapel."[30] It is also worth noting that the plantation accounts for 1723 were repeated at least four times. Many letters were lost, and orders and directions never came through, or if they did, only after months of delay. This hindrance alone caused loss of time and money in building.

Although the contributions hopefully solicited for the building fund and supplies did not continue to pour in as bountifully as they had during the first expansive years, the Society continued its efforts to encourage donations and, from time to time, with some results. In 1721 the Society itself sent windows for the hall and the chapel, steps for the altar piece, and pavement for the chapel.[31] The next year color and oil went into the missionary barrel for painting the outside of the chapel. The Annual Report for 1725 announced that "the Society had sent over all the necessaries for fitting up the chapel, and will proceed to order all the other inside work to be done with all convenient dispatch."[32]

The concentration upon the college buildings, had begun to affect, seriously, the general upkeep on the plantation, and the place badly needed repair. The damage during the heavy rains of 1724 demanded more attention to plantation buildings, and the work on the college building suffered as a result. Money had to be borrowed from the Society to make necessary repairs to the works and to replace equipment. There is a record of £264 paid to John Braithwaite for cattle; of timber purchased to repair the sloop, which had been out of use for two years,[33] and the plantation buildings.[34]

During the third decade of the century little was accomplished toward building the college. It was still unfinished when John Smalridge became ill in 1728, and John Vaughton, his nephew, took over part of the management.[35] However, on his sick bed Smalridge was concerned with the college building, and he wrote the Society not to blame the management of the estates for all the delays that had come. He begged them to instruct the attorneys to proceed with more dispatch; for if the attorneys had been more prompt in their business, he believed the school would have been nearer completion. However, despite his best efforts, the building was still unfinished when Smalridge died in March, 1731.[36]

During these years the attorneys, as representatives of the Society in London, were the plantation's guests, and particular items were marked for their entertainment: an extra cook from another plantation; cases of brandy, arrack, and claret; imported pickles, relishes, and conserves.[37] When it was necessary to hold meetings in Bridgetown, there was further hospitality, for upon the accounts of 1720, stands this item: "Paid for three dinners for the commissioners meeting in Town, 11/16/7½."[38] When we consider that a missionary's salary was ordinarily a mere £50 a year, the expense of these three dinners might seem extravagant.

Always courteous, and kind, Smalridge had no harsh criticism of others in his letters, and his regret was that he could not have accomplished more for the Society. If there was blame, he uncomplainingly took most of it himself. He often reiterated in his letters that if he could make better sugar, the profits would increase, and added that he had earnestly tried to improve his methods. But, hampered by long-distance management, impractical ideas at home and abroad, dilatory and self-seeking attorneys, officious clerics, and a critical community, he nevertheless remained at his task and worked consistently for its accomplishment.

In 1738, although the Society had not yet been able to finish the interior of the chapel because of debts against the estates, it was thought unwise to wait longer for the prosperity that was always just around the corner. Thus the work on the building was resumed. But when the grammar school opened, in the fall of 1745, construction was still unfinished. With this event, not only were the building expenses to be met from the estates, but the additional burden of maintaining the school was laid upon the income.

While the school was being prepared for occupancy, plantation repairs had again lagged, and it was necessary to attend to the inroads of weather upon boiling houses, barns, and shops. In the spring of 1745, Abel Alleyne, plantation manager, resigned because of ill health. John Payne, then well known on the island as a skillful planter with a reputation for truthfulness and honesty, was chosen by the attorneys as Alleyne's successor. The attorneys found things in serious need of repairs,[39] and they decided that the boiling house on the lower plantation would have to be rebuilt. The excessive rains had damaged it.[40]

During this time the teachers at the college chafed under the inconveniences imposed by their unfinished building, particularly when they saw repairs progressing upon the plantation. Indeed, in the revolution by correspondence through which the schoolmasters took over the management of the plantation in 1747, as described in Chapter III, the delay in completing the college buildings was a major charge brought against the management. Thomas Rotherham wrote that even the extremity of renting the plantations might offer a prospect of finishing the college buildings, but as matters stood, the plantation absorbed all the time, energy, and money of the management.[41]

Aroused by the information received from these men lately sent from England, the Society wrote its attorneys to proceed to finish the college. Payne was directed to answer that the Society's orders would be carried out. He replied that he had noted the directions regarding the college, and as soon as the attorneys ordered he would set about "cheerfully and vigorously to finish it." But he assured the Society:

... it could never have happened at a worse time. ... lumber of all sorts are at a most extravagant price near double as usual which will appear by the account ... There will be a great quantity of both planks and boards as well as several feet of hard timber wanting to finish the college. It will much enhance the expense to purchase the several materials at this so extraordinary rate.[42]

In an earlier letter Payne had given another reason for not going ahead with the building. There had been a blast on the sugar cane, and "several long spells of dry weather in the most prime months for the cane to grow" had cut down the prospects for a profitable sugar crop.[43]

Joseph Bewsher, one of the schoolmasters, suggested that John Payne live on the upper plantation, where good quarters were already built. A great deal of trouble such as confused accounts of college and plantation living expenses would then be avoided.[44] William Bryant, professor of philosophy and mathematics, who had come out in the spring of 1747, added his pen to the controversy. He placed considerable blame upon the attorneys for retarding progress, and wrote that the faculty had

... expected them at last to give special directions for fitting up the chapel, which is greatly wanted, but they refuse to give any farther orders about finishing the college. They acknowledged they had instructions from the Society for doing this. . . . [pleading the] prodigious price of all materials which they say the Society are strangers to. This would be plausible if we didn't have practically all the materials. The coving of the chapel is done already and only wants painting, for which it is in danger of being spoiled. There is marble provided for the floor, and the windows were put in some time ago.[45]

Such complaints as these, well-enforced by apparent facts, came through to the Society, and the incumbent management was not able to meet them with convincing evidence to the contrary. Thus the schoolmasters, with their greater literary abilities, won in this contest by correspondence.

However, these young men, lately from the halls of Oxford or Cambridge, shortly found that there were more difficulties to be surmounted than appeared on the surface. Busy with their new responsibilities, they wrote more and more of conditions at the sugar house, of the price of cane and slaves, and the problems of hiring a proper manager, and less and less of the building program.[46] By 1760, the Bishop of St. Asaph reported that he was "really amazed at our . . . . immoderate charge" of more than £12,000 for the still uncompleted buildings. Although the south side of the college was finished, there were no floors in one of the wings, and the roof was "much out of repair." In view of the delay, he recommended that the original design planned around a quadrangle be abandoned, and efforts be concentrated on completing the main building as it stood.[47]

When the school was closed for financial reasons in 1775, repairs and completion of the buildings were abandoned. The hurricane of 1780 greatly damaged part of the college structure although the loss was not so severe as in some of the other plantation buildings.[48] By 1795, however, with all debts in Barbados and London discharged, and the buildings partly restored, the Society once again determined "to proceed in the repairs of the College almost destroyed by the last Hurricane, which are already begun, and will be carried on with all expedition."[49]

With the continued prosperity on the estates, beginning about this time, the college buildings received their share of attention, especially as repairs were required to meet the needs of the growing school. In 1819 the wooden chapel serving the estate was destroyed by a minor hurricane, and was replaced by a stone structure in 1821.[50] The new impetus toward completion of the college project supplied by the appointment of a bishop for Barbados, in 1824, combined with the more than adequate funds in the treasury, gave rise to a second large building program, somewhat comparable to that of the first decade of construction under Smalridge.

Shortly after his arrival in Barbados, in 1825, Bishop William Hart Coleridge visited Codrington College and began plans for its expansion.

I have only just time to enclose for your Lordship's inspection a plan for the enlargement of Codrington College. The dark lines represent the portion of building at present standing and partially occupied; the red lines the proposed addition. The College is itself beautifully situated in a secluded and healthy and romantic spot near the sea and is a much finer building than I had expected; it cost if I am rightly informed not less than £20,000 sterling in its erection—the proposed addition would I have reason to hope, fall considerably within that sum for the present building was erected at a very expensive time, and under the care of Commissioners sent from England—No additions will be required to the Principal's Lodge which was Col. Codrington's own residence, and is an excellent and respectable mansion. The Hall and Chapel and present apartments require only repairs or alteration in their arrangements. The building corresponding to the Principal's Lodge would at once complete the front, and remove the under managers house, and the negro yard, which on *many accounts,* ought not to be so near to the college. The Student apartments beyond on either side toward the sea are so placed as to admit of a free current of air pervading all the buildings. . . .

The college when seen from the Society's Chapel on the hill above or the Chapel seen from the College below on its broken and woody eminence, with the fine avenue of cabbage trees leading to the college, form equally very beautiful objects and the country around is broken and romantic. I mention these points as I have never seen any account that does justice either to the situation of the college in point of beauty or health, or comfort, or to the present buildings, and these are capable of enlargement and improvement at an expence which I should trust that the funds of the Institution might bear.[51]

Under the guidance of the energetic Bishop, the building program made rapid progress and by July, 1830, shortly before the formal opening of the college as an advanced institution of learning, John Pinder, the Principal, reported that the completion of the whole plant awaited only the work to be done on some sixteen student apartments, which should be ready by Christmas. The entire college plant, when finished, would include a hall, a chapel and a library, with living accommodations for thirty students and a suite of rooms for the tutors.[52]

The college hardly had got under way when another hurricane descended in 1831, and the slow business of rebuilding was begun: an eventuality which finally caused the harassed Society to form a "Hurricane and Contingencies Fund."[53] It may be noted that in 1834, before the buildings in Barbados had been completely restored, an engraving of the first Codrington Chapel was used as a guide for the design of a church building at Muswell Brook, New South Wales.[54]

In common with all phases of the Codrington project, the task of housing the college was, then, one of delay, discouragement, and disaster, but always in the background lay the firm purpose to achieve a set goal. Perhaps this intangible quality is best expressed by a writer who, after describing the great fire which destroyed most of the college buildings in 1926, added the comment: "The blow might have seemed irreparable, but in the British Colonies it is not the habit to allow *Troja fuit* to be said of such an institution as Codrington College."[55]

CHAPTER III

Of the Plantations Intire: concerning the Conduct of
Affairs; of the managers; the town agents; the sugar
merchants; the works and utensils; of great Trouble
and Expence and finally, of growing Prosperity and
Zeal in the Management of the Estates.

By JOHN A. SCHUTZ and MAUD E. O'NEIL

THE MANAGEMENT of overseas property, in which the separation between owner and manager plays so great a part, was a problem not only of the Society for the Propagation of the Gospel as absentee owner of a West Indian sugar plantation, but of every Englishman interested in overseas enterprise. Even great property owners like Charles Ellis and John Gladstone, whose instructions on humane management were usually ignored by their agents, were subjected to vexatious delays, misunderstandings, and the hundred other difficulties which arose from long-distance management. Keen competition existed among the islands of the West Indies and between English and foreign-owned islands. The local managers of the plantations throughout the Lesser Antilles were convinced that humane programs meant deficits for which they would be blamed. The manager wished to educate, not the slaves, but the bishops and other members of the Society who knew nothing of sugar, or the tropics, or the control of "unseasoned" labor. Occasionally a bishop read the literature on sugar culture until he became an "absentee" scholar on the subject.

OF THE PLANTATIONS INTIRE

WITH THE Codrington estates actually in its possession, the Society's first considerations were to determine as accurately as possible the material wealth accruing from the land and to begin operating the plantations. To secure exact information, the Secretary dispatched letters to the attorneys in Barbados and to John Smalridge, manager of the Codrington estates. By December, 1712, ten months after the title had been cleared and nearly two and one-half years after Codrington's death, the London members had enough data available to survey the potentialities of the property.[1]

The two plantations in Barbados were known as Codrington and Consetts. The former, consisting of 270 acres, three-fourths of which was arable and highly cultivable, was the smaller and occupied the higher ground. Terraces linked Codrington to the lower plantation of Consetts, situated at the base of a thousand-foot cliff. The greater part of Consett's 480 acres was rocky and suitable principally for pasturage.[2] But this plantation included Consetts harbor, a valuable asset since it permitted coastwise shipping of sugar and supplies. By a fair road the two plantations were about fourteen miles from Bridgetown, the chief island harbor. Distances were not great in Barbados, for the island formed a compact little triangle, fourteen miles wide and twenty-one miles in length, and its circumference of fifty-five miles gave easy access to the sea. However, the entire coastal stretch of Barbados afforded few harbors even for small sloops and a growing atoll reef near the coast made navigation hazardous. Shipments of plantation products had to travel coastwise or by poor inland roads to Bridgetown, there to be transshipped to ocean-going vessels.

The Society was justified in its early optimism over the material resources of the Codrington estates. In 1712 and for a period thereafter, conditions were normal, a one-crop sugar economy was well established, and prices were fair. However, it was evident from the first that if profits were to be realized from the plantation, proper management must be secured and immediate action taken to restore the run-down lands to maximum production by repairing the

---

[1] For notes to chap. iii, see pp. 130–133.

damage suffered from slack operation during the months of litigation.[3]

The problems which confronted the Society as absentee owner of a West Indian sugar plantation were many. Sometimes, to the men in Barbados, they seemed insuperable. But the special value of the Codrington records lies in their continuation over a century, thus showing how, by trial and error, methods of long-distance management were evolved. Transport by slow sailing vessels delayed crops and correspondence and resulted in confusion in the operation of the estates;[4] immediate decisions were rendered impossible, adequate investigations impractical, and losses were incurred that might otherwise have been avoided. Injudicious decisions often resulted in misunderstandings and in discouragement of those entrusted with the actual burden of management. Opportunities were also afforded for unscrupulous men to take advantage of the distant owners to turn the fluctuating profits of the business to their own advantage.

Long-distance management required a complex hierarchy of attorneys, agents, and managers, who were required to make their reports to the Society in writing. The London office participated actively in plantation affairs, and usually retained the power of final decision in vital matters. But the success or the failure of the plantation management rested, in large part, with the Barbadian attorneys. The first attorneys were, as has been seen, appointed by the Society during the litigation over the will to serve as representatives on the scene. In the same way attorneys were appointed to conduct plantation affairs. Usually they were wealthy sugar growers or Anglican ministers. They were required by the Society to meet frequently if occasion demanded, to keep a record of these meetings faithfully, and to send the minutes to London for the information of the owners. As trustees, they were permitted to act very freely in routine matters, yet at times the Society made searching investigations and advised them on even the most minute points of plantation operation.

One of the powers usually delegated to the attorneys was that of selecting the plantation manager, the key man in making a success of the project. The duties of the manager were very exacting. He had to reconcile the specific orders of the Barbadian attorneys with the plans of the London Society, meet the actual problems of management, and show a profit at the end of the season. He was required to attend the meetings of the attorneys, although he was not always one of them. He recommended improvements upon the plantations and additions to the labor force. His reports were recorded in the minutes.

It was convenient for the Codrington plantations, which were fourteen miles from Bridgetown, to engage agents to handle their town business. Prices fluctuated, commodities deteriorated, and bills of exchange were often difficult to obtain. Shipping was uncertain, the arrival of boats unpredictable, and cargoes were often badly damaged. For outgoing shipments, boats had to be secured that would insure the safe arrival of goods with the least delay and minimum expense. The profits and losses of a plantation depended to a considerable extent upon the successful handling of the incoming and outgoing goods by the town agent. He was in a position to turn things to his own advantage, and the Codrington business enabled him to manage his own affairs more profitably. As a rule the agent had some occupation of his own in town and frequently he served as agent for several plantations. If possible, the manager of an estate arranged to act as his own town agent.

The Rev. Arthur Holt's correspondence with the Bishop of London included a lengthy discussion of the agent's functions.[5] Realizing that the Society might not have a full understanding of how this office was conducted, Holt wrote:

The agent, if he is a merchant in town, receives the rum from the plantation, which is otherwise ready money. Orders are drawn upon him as occasions require, to pay off the workmen, to discharge the levys, etc. The longer he can put off the payment of such orders, the greater advantage he makes to himself. When he is called upon for provisions, it is at his option to order the refuse of his store at his own price to the plantation. These things, with the commissions he has for buying the rum, for selling his provisions, and lumber, and the advantage of putting off his own cask, besides a salary, make a town agency worth any merchant's while to strive for. He that is an attorney to several estates may engage a town agent to do the business for his own in a most diligent manner for little or nothing. But if the manager has that agency in his own hands, the merchants will buy the rum for ready cash, which the manager will have in hand, to discharge any expenses of the estate, and when provisions or other necessaries are wanting, the manager goes to town and purchases the best at a ready money price, which is Barbadoes.[6]

The upkeep of buildings and the maintenance of equipment was always an expensive item in the plantation accounts. The tropical climate was disastrous to the buildings, for the heavy rains washed out foundations, hurricanes tore off roofs and swept away flimsy structures, and heat and dampness caused the timber to decay. Repairs were always in order, for, as Joseph Bewsher wrote in 1747, "no sooner is one Building repaired but another is ready to fall."[7] The boiling house, repaired and reconstructed yearly, showed the effect of the constant inroads of the weather. However, the upkeep of the housing might have been comparatively inexpensive if the Society had not been forced to buy within a restricted market. Lumber was unusually scarce in Barbados, and particularly so during periods of war. In 1746, for example, the attorneys reported that lumber prices had risen nearly 100 per cent.

Certainly not least among the problems of management was that of growing sugar cane and shipping the finished product to England, which is discussed in the next chapter. Fortunately, the plantations did not rely solely upon sugar to meet expenses. Ordinarily, rum and molasses, the by-products of sugar making, could be depended upon to defray the running costs.[8] Of course, these products were dependent upon the success of the estates in growing sugar cane and in maintaining the equipment necessary to manufacture it. The Society also had nearly 300 acres which could be planted in guinea corn, although the managers could not always utilize this acreage to its maximum extent. Guinea corn was usually an important item in the food of the Negro and the operating costs of the plantation could be lessened on a self-sustaining economy. As early as March 23, 1711, John Smalridge had demonstrated his awareness of the importance of this crop, for he wrote his brother in London concerning the "want of Corn, or Breadkind, as we call it here, for our Slaves." Smalridge added:

...after this year I have taken care to prevent it [a shortage]; except a Common Calamity happens. We used to have in their Master's time such supplys from abroad, but I have taken care to Plant, and will give encouragement to the Slaves to do the same: It is the greatest misfortune in this Island that few Planters give them a Belly full and the reason is this: their Numb[rs] are so great and Corn so dear, that they can't afford it; that Master that gives his Slave a pint of Corn for one day, thinks him well provided for.[9]

Next to the problem of long-distance management, the most difficult for the Society was the maintenance of an adequate number
of Negroes. If the estates were understocked with slaves less sugar
was grown, the costs of operation became exceedingly high, repairs
on the buildings were generally neglected, and the ledger recorded
inevitable losses.[10] General Codrington had stipulated that the
Society should keep 300 Negroes on the estates. But this number
was not always maintained. When the plantations were turned
over to the Society in 1712, there were only 276 Negroes. However,
the number of slaves does not, of course, tally with the count of
field hands, for allowance must be made for the very young and
the aged.

In the very early years the slave population was almost equally
divided between males and females. In 1758 a complete list of the
Negroes contained twenty-five past the age of labor.[11] Three methods were used in maintaining a full complement of Negroes; hiring
them, encouraging them to breed, and buying them from the local
markets.

The practice of hiring Negroes, followed by the managers
throughout the century, occasioned considerable controversy.
Sometimes they were rented from neighboring plantations; sometimes, as in the case of Grant Elcock, a manager brought with him
a large group of slaves who were rented to the Society at an agreed
price.[12] In one year the Society might pay out £1,200 for rented
labor of this type. From time to time, throughout the eighteenth
century, the Society was told by its Barbadian representatives that
the purchase of slaves, who represented capital, was far cheaper
in the long run.[13] As will appear later, the high costs for Negro hire
were the determining factor in the purchase of the Henley plantation in 1766 for the sole purpose of obtaining more slaves.

In the eighteenth century the Negro birth rate at Codrington
was extremely low. Mortality among Negro children was high on
sugar estates. From time to time the managers wrote despairingly
to London that they were doing everything in their power to encourage the slaves to be more prolific. Only the will of a perverse
Providence, they suggested, accounted for their failure in this
direction. Later in the century special inducements were offered
to Negro mothers, a sum of 6s. 3d. being awarded as a bonus. The

plantation accounts list payments of a similar amount to midwives and make provision for castor oil for the babies.[14]

As for the purchase of slaves, agents buying them at Bridgetown had to be on the alert, since the market for good Negroes was highly competitive.[15] Even the slave for common labor was difficult to obtain. Few plantation owners purchased many African, or green Negroes as they were known, at any one time, because the training period of assimilation into the general plantation routine was long and unprofitable.[16] Replacements sapped a large part of the revenues of the estates; in 1761 the market price on slaves ran from £38 to £75 a head.[17] When groups were purchased, the attorneys wrote, "No certain proportion of the Sexes is in general observed . . . tho' 'tis usually judged most eligible to have a superior number of Females," chiefly because of the issue.[18]

In addition to the fact that an insufficient number of Negroes meant a decrease in production on the plantation, there was the matter of the special skills which could not be developed if the slaves were forced to spend all their time in the field. By 1762 the Negroes who had learned trades under the regime of Christopher Codrington were all dead and their skills had not been acquired by the young Negroes. Arrangements were, therefore, made to apprentice some young slaves as carpenters, masons, and blacksmiths.[19] The attorneys in 1761 recommended that twenty-five Negroes be trained for this job and retained always in the pot house, regardless of the need for them in other work.[20]

In acquiring the Codrington estates, the Society inherited, as well, all the problems of operating a West Indian sugar plantation. Throughout the century the London office was concerned with proper personnel for the complicated structure of management and marketing. For the men in Barbados, the problem was to maintain the equipment and labor force, to interpret local conditions and practices in terms understandable to absentee owners, and to show a profit on the books. The early difficulties of adjustment, and the ultimate success in working out practicable procedures are best shown in a chronological account of the plantation in operation.

During the first two years of wearisome litigation over the will, the estates had run down. Fences had been broken by the wind and

rotted by dampness. The buildings had gradually fallen apart and
slaves had died.[21] But with the Society in possession, repairs were
immediately undertaken under the efficient direction of John
Smalridge. Smalridge had acted as bookkeeper of the plantations
for Christopher Codrington and knew the plantations well. By
1714 the Society could boast of having one of the best-equipped
sugar works in Barbados. Broken fences had been rebuilt with the
sturdy timbers given by Colonel William Codrington. Roofs torn
by storm and wind had been repaired; slave quarters, mills, boiling
houses, and manager's dwellings had been reconstructed. In fact,
most of the repairs of a serious nature had been made, and by careful economy the attorneys and manager had kept within their
budget. Bumper crops were being raised and sugar prices were
high.[22]

During this period of early prosperity plans for the college were
pushed forward with vigor. But the hard times which hit the whole
of Barbados beginning in 1718 were reflected in the affairs of the
Codrington estates where the account books carried, in addition
to plantation expenses, the costs of an ambitious building program.
By 1724, a wet year, the declining income from the estates called
for retrenchment. As in other times of plantation depression, one
of the biggest problems during this period was the insufficient supply of Negroes.[23] In making a survey of plantation labor since 1702,
Smalridge concluded that he did not have enough slaves to operate
successfully no matter how favorable conditions might be, and he
suggested to the Society that the quota of Negroes be increased by
a program of annual purchase. The losses in Negroes each year had
usually exceeded the ten he had been delegated to buy, and thus
the supply had constantly diminished.[24]

The Society lost twenty-nine Negroes during the wet year of
1724, because of poor housing conditions and exposure to the
weather.[25] The heavy work also contributed to this epidemic of
illness and death, since night shifts as well as day shifts had to be
maintained in the boiling houses, and mortality was high among
the Negroes who worked at night.[26] Likewise, continuous labor in
the cane fields was detrimental to the health of "the Society's
family," particularly on the lower plantation where the atmosphere was very humid and two or three degrees hotter than on the

upper plantation. Negroes carried the cane up the steep slope of the plateau to the boiling houses, and this arduous work brought about an increasingly high death rate among them.[27]

At such times of distress the struggle between the idealism of the Society's program and the materialism necessary for its realization was heightened, particularly for the harassed manager. Thus John Smalridge, in reporting Gilbert Ramsay's bequest of £100 and his books to the Codrington estates in 1728, added wistfully, "I wish he had given his Negroes—they would have been very serviceable under our present Circumstances, for I believe we shall not be able to do much except the number was made up according to the will of the Donor and one good seasoned Negro is worth two bought."[28]

To obtain an adequate number of Negroes it had usually been necessary to purchase unseasoned slaves, for the others were scarce in the open market. Also, the seasoning of green slaves was an expensive process and the introduction of these new members into the group increased restlessness and insubordination among the old plantation Negroes. Runaways were more frequent, and, aside from the loss of labor during the runaway's absence, there was the expense incurred in retrieving him; for a good sum of money was paid to the person catching and returning a fugitive.[29] Occasionally an especially recalcitrant Negro was sold, but this form of punishment seems to have been used largely to impress the others. In July, 1728, Smalridge reported that he hoped "the rumor of shipping will make some of them mend their manners."[30]

After the death of Smalridge, in March, 1730, the plantation entered a decade of misfortune, beginning with disagreement among the attorneys and renewed trouble over the town agent. Moreover, this fourth decade of the century ushered in a series of bad years for Barbados. In August, 1731, a severe storm struck the island and the Codrington plantations did not escape. However, the mills stood, although the repairs on the other buildings amounted to more than £200. Because of crop shortages and other calamities, the estates were not able to keep up their supply of Negroes or to pay necessary salaries, and were forced to borrow money from the Society for their operating expenses. The general economic situation throughout the island was desperate. Many persons left Barbados for the Carolinas and other places on the American continent, and the value of property declined rapidly.[31] Commodities were scarce, and bills of exchange were difficult to get. In 1732 the Rev. William Johnson, who was serving as one of the Codrington attorneys, cited an instance of paying 32 per cent for a bill of exchange sent to the Society.[32] Shipping space was difficult to secure because captains refused cargoes.

The tense political situation which developed in Barbados, as a result of this depression, is reflected in the plantation records. For the Codrington attorneys voted to join the majority of the planters in refusing to pay the government's levy on their slaves.[33] The Rev. Arthur Holt was the only member of the board of attorneys who sided with the governor. On November 17, 1730, in a letter to the Bishop of London, he questioned the motives of his fellow attorneys in a bitter paragraph:

Mr. Osborn is a man whose religion we know not. He was just a servant worth nothing, after that a manager and attorney to several estates, and has found means to make himself master of more wind mill estates than any gentleman in Barbados. Mr. Bennet will be better known when he has settled accounts with the Assiento Company, and done justice to his wife's children one of which is now at law with him for about fifteen thousand pounds.[34]

To the other attorney, Abel Alleyne, he gave a clean bill of character, except that Alleyne had joined in the faction against the governor. On April 6, 1731, under orders from the Society, the attorneys paid the required taxes, but recorded in their minutes that they were not in sympathy with the order because it would antagonize the other planters on the island.[35]

Although he was consistently outvoted by the other attorneys, Holt continued his campaign and when a vacancy occurred on the board, he suggested the name of the Rev. William Johnson, a friend of Governor Henry Worsley.[36] Again the Society accepted his recommendation and named Johnson. There seems to have been no question in London about Holt's devotion to the welfare of the Society's estates and, if he questioned the other attorneys' motives, it may sometimes have been for good cause. For in one letter he wrote, "I am perhaps the more upon my guard, for hearing an attorney, who since is dead, with a seeming complacency predict that these estates would soon be reduced to the necessity of being sold or ruined, and he gave but too plain hints that he should be glad to be the purchaser."[37]

Another altercation arose in July, 1731, when Holt asked for a careful examination of the accounts, whereupon Bennett flew into a rage and threatened Holt's life. In his letter to Edmund Gibson, Bishop of London, Holt quoted Bennett as saying, "The Society was obliged to him, and he had a good mind to serve them no more. Both he and Mr. Osborne reflected that from the other estates to which they were attorneys they received the advantage of commissions, but by the Society's estates they got nothing."[38] However, in spite of the quarrel, the accounts were taken care of in the accustomed manner, and nothing detrimental either to Bennett's or Osborne's reputation was noted.

Although Holt wrote frequently to London, he did not always receive the unqualified support of the Society, as is illustrated in a matter concerning the Bridgetown agency. In the early days of Smalridge's management, the Society had employed a town agent there, but a difficulty arose in the accounts which resulted in Smalridge himself taking over the post.[39] On his death, there were many contenders for the place and, although his nephew, John Vaughton, acting manager of the plantation, assumed the agency in 1730, there were plans on foot to award the position to James Pemberton. Holt protested, charging that Pemberton's former conduct of the business had been detrimental to the estates. But the other attorneys prevailed, Vaughton was displaced, and Pemberton obtained the position at an annual salary of £50. According to Holt, the stage was thus set for further questionable acts against the plantation.[40]

In spite of all the difficulties and misfortunes of this period, the plantations, at the end of the decade, were able to pay off the debt they owed the Society. Vaughton's management, during this difficult period, brought early commendation from the Rev. Mr. Holt, who observed that "for sobriety, diligence, and skillfulness in business, his good Christian life, and his zeal for the instruction of the slaves," he was well qualified for the position entrusted to him by the Society. Somewhat later, however, during the height of his feud with the other attorneys, Holt accused Vaughton of selfish interests in favoring his own Negroes, which were hired out to the Codrington estates. For, as he wrote, "the manager gets above a hundred pounds yearly by keeping his own Negroes upon the estates (of which I heard him say he never lost one) who may do the easiest work, eat the plantation provisions, and improve in strength and number, whilst the others are worn out with the hardest labour."[41]

As was its practice when such charges were brought, the Society took pains to hear both sides of the story before making a decision in the matter. In such investigations, the accused party was informed of the charges brought against him, and requested to give his own explanation. If possible, the opinions of other residents of the community, familiar with the situation, were obtained. In this case, Vaughton was retained as manager, with a special admonition from the Society regarding his responsibility for the well-being of the Negroes.

If absentee management was difficult before, it was doubly difficult when the grammar school, sometimes called "the College," began functioning in 1745. New thorny questions came up in connection with school affairs. Sometimes the attorneys seemed dilatory in solving these problems, and they were unjustly blamed when in reality they were not able to act without authorization which was not always forthcoming from the Society in London. One year after the school started, the attorneys, hard pressed with their new tasks, wrote the Society rather pointedly that they did the best they could, but the Society was negligent in answering them. For, as they wrote, "without this supposition, so long a silence on the subject which seemed before to have engaged the attention of the Society would not easily be accounted for."[42]

In addition to the other problems of the attorneys there was trouble with the faculty. Not one of the schoolmasters was represented on the board of attorneys. They were called into meetings when a specific school problem arose, but they were dismissed as soon as they had presented it. It was not long before the smouldering resentment of the faculty broke into open flame. The professors felt that they were being ignored, and in letters to London, charged that lack of representation in affairs that concerned the school was detrimental to its success. From their comfortable quarters they had, moreover, observed numerous instances of mismanagement on the estates which they did not hesitate to outline. As a result, in 1747, the Society added Bryant and Rotheram to its list of attorneys, and from this date until 1751 the schoolmasters were dominant.[43]

With all the energy of new proprietors, the gentlemen of the schoolroom began their work as attorneys. They were known in England as pious and scholarly men, and had been interviewed in London only a few years previously for the positions they held in the school. Their work there had been commendable, considering the limited means at their disposal. They were now called upon to employ some of their skill in the operation of a sugar plantation.

Their first action, as might be expected, was to check the power of the manager, John Payne, and he, with his family, was transferred to the upper estate. His removal gave the schoolmasters more freedom of action in college affairs and permitted them to discuss more easily the problems of plantation operation. A careful investigation of Payne's books and the records of the bookkeeper revealed many inaccuracies. Both men were, therefore, called to the college to explain their entries. A rather meticulous hearing was given them, and their explanations were brushed aside as inadequate or, as one attorney expressed it, as "frivolous." William Bryant, the professor of mathematics, was assigned the general supervision of the accounts, and he promised to have the books regularly posted. This latter action was taken to remove "the bad impressions people had concieved in regard to the credit of the Society's plantations for these two years past."[44] Some months later John Payne was dismissed for misconduct.[45]

The instructors then set out to investigate the general conditions of the plantation and the buildings. The still house was falling apart and "would occasion a great deficiency in the rum toward answering the expense for the year." The smith's shop, the cooper's shop, the pot house, and the kiln equally needed repair; consequently the professors drew £300 in addition to the £1,000 borrowed the previous year.[46] These repairs were near completion in 1750 when they purchased a half interest in a sloop to transport more efficiently the estate's produce to Bridgetown, or, as they reported, because it was "deemed necessary, that we be masters of our time of carrying our goods from the Plantation to Bridgetown."[47]

In 1753 the professors appointed Grant Elcock as sole manager of the estates to replace a Mr. Kettlewell and a Mr. Say, who had divided the plantations between them for management, but were unable to bring the desired profits.[48] Elcock was a man of character, ability, and experience. But even more to recommend him was the large gang of Negroes he brought with him. He was paid £200 annually for his own services, a higher figure than the former managers received, in addition to what he received as rent for his Negroes.[49] But the attorneys justified this additional expenditure on the ground that no matter how fine an estate the Society possessed, maximum profits could not be expected without an experienced manager. After six months of his service, the professors were able to report that the gentlemen of Barbados had remarked that the properties "have not been under so good management for many years."[50]

This temporary success proved illusory. For during the period 1749 to 1757 only 70 hogsheads of sugar were produced yearly, and not more than 120 acres of land were utilized annually. The average profits were £234, but after all charges for improvement on the properties and maintenance of the college were deducted, the Society found a total deficit of £5,482 for these years. So far as the Society was concerned, the professors had not materially altered the financial position of the estates.[51] The only visible result of their management was that they no longer complained of the attorney's activities and that they found the complexities of plantation operation more than an academic matter. They lost interest in managing the estates and withdrew from their offices as attorneys.

Since all past attempts to manage the properties successfully had met with only reasonable success the Society in London decided, in 1760, to make a more thorough investigation of conditions there. A special committee was appointed which included the energetic Robert Hay Drummond, Bishop of St. Asaph; former Lieutenant Governor Robert Dinwiddie of Virginia; and John Pownall, Secretary of the Board of Trade.[52] After some weeks of consideration, they recommended that the Society purchase seasoned Negroes to bring the stock to a total of 300. If seasoned Negroes could not be purchased, Africans were to be bought, provided the number was not above 20 yearly.[53] The Bishop of St. Asaph was the most active of the committeemen, and the most outspoken. In a report to the Archbishop of Canterbury, he observed: "When I reflect . . . I see enough of our Indolence or Inexperience to account for all our failures."[54]

Meanwhile in Barbados the attorneys were making an inquiry of their own. Their one important conclusion, which agreed substantially with the London report, read: "The great Failure of the Society's Estates are certainly owing, principally, to their not being fully stocked."[55] Thus the increase of the labor force was the first step in the return to profitable production. To supply the necessary numbers for immediate production the attorneys urged an outlay of £8,000 to £10,000 for the purchase of 106 Negroes. Even with this great expenditure, an additional 106 Negroes were required if the Society desired maximum returns from the estates.[56]

The task of securing a large group of well-seasoned Negroes was not an easy one. To solve the problem, the attorneys suggested the purchase of another plantation, fully stocked, the property to be resold but the slaves retained. Suppose, wrote the attorneys, such an estate could be purchased for £20,000 Barbados currency (£14,000 sterling), the interest of 6 per cent would not exceed the sums paid out annually for the hire of Negroes. The land could then be sold, in small or large sections, to reduce the indebtedness. And the Codrington estates would acquire the necessary number of seasoned hands.[57]

With the Society's approval of this plan, the attorneys completed the purchase of the neighboring Henley estate in 1766, paying £13,333 sterling.[58] The following year the lands were sold to Gedney Clarke who agreed to pay £11,011 for them.[59] The attorneys were embarrassed when Clarke went bankrupt and failed to complete his payments to the Society. His bankruptcy occurred when the inspector general of customs seized Henley in 1774 to compensate the government for £10,000 delinquency in the accounts of Gedney Clarke as collector of customs in Barbados.[60] The Society was at first inclined to hold the men responsible, who, in 1767, had neglected to register properly the documents of sale. This failure also served to keep the Society from repossessing the Henley property until 1783. It was sold for £5,000 to John Poyer in 1788.[61]

The American Revolution was extremely destructive of profits from the plantation, as will appear in more detail in the next chapter. In 1780 a devastating hurricane again visited the island, and changed "the luxuriant spring . . . in this one night to the dreariest winter . . ."[62] As for the Society's plantations, Sir John Gay Alleyne and the Rev. Michael Mashart reported to London that "most of the buildings on the estate have been blown down, except the mills, but not one negroe lost, and a very few cattle in proportion to the number on the Estates; the mansion [was] entirely uncovered, the walls alone standing, and a part of the College . . . [was] greatly damaged."[63]

In the meanwhile, the Society decided to relieve the situation by permitting the attorneys in Barbados to draw from the general funds of the corporation. The sum was to be paid back to them as soon as the estates were again able to make sufficient profits. In 1781 the debt to the Society amounted to £3,332, and the estates were in a run-down condition. By 1783 the financial position of the plantations had become critical. The only solution that remained was to rent the property, a plan which had been under discussion for some forty years. But there had been considerable opposition to this plan, both in Barbados and in London. There were rumors of undesirable tenants who had ruined plantations by failure to repair buildings, by neglecting to replenish stock, and by working slaves to death. In 1777 the attorneys had argued that a shrewd and self-seeking tenant would exploit the resources of the land and leave a worn-out estate.[64] The Society had been warned that the slaves would become restless with a change of managers, and the good work of Christianizing them would have to be discontinued, and the grammar school, which depended upon the estates for its fresh vegetables, services in transportation, and the use of Negroes, would become more costly in operation.[65]

In 1775 the financial situation had become so desperate that the school was closed, and the Society determined to rent the estates. The contract of 1783 provided for a rental of £500 a year and the profits were to be donated to the Society.[66] In February, 1783, this proposal was accepted by John Braithwaite.[67] His years of management of the estates, which terminated in 1793, were very profitable to the Society, as appears in the annual accounts listed in Chapter

IV. The yield from the estates increased yearly, until Braithwaite could boast of £1,953 Barbados currency as an average annual clearance. By 1793 he had realized profits for the Society amounting to £19,533.[68]

Money from the plantations came in freely. Debts were cleared and the building of the greater Codrington College was in the offing when, in 1793, the Society prepared to assume again the operation of the estates. Braithwaite was congratulated for his energy and rewarded with a beautiful piece of plate. Indeed, leasing the plantations had long-term results for the Society in the following years. The days of severe deficits were over.[69]

Upon the retirement of John Braithwaite as lessee in 1793, and the appointment of Edward Clarke as manager, the Society itself entered a period of more efficient plantation operation. In the first ten years the estates cleared £12,358, a handsome profit, although it was £7,000 less than Braithwaite had cleared in his ten years of management. From 1804 to 1813, inclusive, the cane crops were large but, although the average annual clearance was £1,104, the price of provisions in Barbados was exorbitant, and the expenses of the revived grammar school exceeded returns from the estates by £2,150.[70] Yet the Society's position was a comparatively happy one, for in some of the West Indian islands, and particularly Jamaica, one-fourth of the sugar estates had been either abandoned or sold.[71]

Some of the credit for the good conditions at Codrington in the period after 1813 must be given to the agricultural manager, Thomas Hollingsworth, who was appointed in 1813 and to his successor, Forster Clarke, who served from 1815 to 1834. Their duties were chiefly concerned with keeping the production of sugar at a maximum level. Not only were their responsibilities thus limited, but their incomes depended upon the profits that were received from the cane. They were allowed a 5 per cent commission of the net proceeds.[72] They superintended the care of the Negroes and saw to the repair of the buildings.

The most profitable years yet recorded for the plantation were those from 1814 to 1824 when nearly £3,840 were cleared each year. The total receipts were more than £40,000, and expenditures were £27,800. These long-awaited dividends were clear profits, and in addition the Society had put aside funds for replacement and repairs.[73] A glance at the plantation accounts for one of these years reveals a tremendous outlay for education, equipment, salaries, and general improvements. In 1818 the plantations had a total income of £8,648, of which sugar accounted for 74 per cent of the total, or £6,396, whereas only 8 per cent, or £716, was realized from rum and molasses. Cooperage and the sale of vegetables, milk, and other plantation products accounted for the remainder of the income.[74]

As for the money expenditures for operation, the 1818 report shows £3,058 expended for provisions, repairs, and salaries. This sum includes £494 for Negroes, £108 for supplies for white labor, £236 for repairs, and £241 for the hire of 1,921 days' labor by a gang of Negroes and for fertilizing the plantations.[75] The maintenance of the school was a costly item, for £1,870 was used to instruct the foundation students, for Negro training, for repairs, and for general expenditures. The master received a salary of £266 and £640 for the expenses of twelve foundation students. The charge for repairs, £126, was not great, considering the large outlay in the past. When all the expenditures, including those of the college, had been taken into account a profit of £2,500 remained.[76]

The Society was able to make a profit during the years after 1813 for a number of reasons. First, the price of sugar was high. In 1814 muscovado sugar sold in London for as much as 91 shillings per hundredweight. Second, there was an adequate supply of Negro laborers. Negroes numbered 411 in July, 1834. Third, the plantations were well stocked with cattle. Fourth, greater efforts were made to keep the buildings in repair. Fifth, better business methods had been introduced by agricultural managers who served on a commission basis. Sixth, transportation was not so great a hazard as in the days of George II. The years of war were over, more shipping space was available, and travel between England and Barbados was more regular and frequent.[77]

CHAPTER IV

Of the Produce of the Plantations; the time and season
of Planting and Reaping of Canes; of the Labour force,
of Rum and Molasses; the Sugar Account and the
Actual Neat Clearances of the Estates.

By HAZEL MORSE HARTLEY

CROPS IN THE eighteenth century were grown on the basis of folk knowledge. Father taught son in the fields. A Dutch windmill was not built from a blueprint, but out of the builder's experience. The Codrington reports are from the ledger of the grower. They include accounts of the weather, experiments with the soil, pests, the process of sugar making, marketing, the "seasoning" of new laborers, the price of slaves, the problems of storage, of commissions, of shipping, and finally of sale in distant markets. The processes of sugar production, the hazards of blast, of hurricane, of extreme variations in seasonal rainfall, of fire, were those of plantation economy in Barbados, and are, of course, similar to those of growers in the West Indies today. Adam Smith declared that Britain had sent more wealth to the West Indies than was ever returned to her. This opinion was not the prevailing view, and the islands were regarded as the jewels of the Empire; that is, as producers of wealth, the nursery of seamen and of the Navy.

The details of the processes of sugar production are difficult to secure, and for that reason Codrington's records are particularly valuable.

OF THE PRODUCE OF THE PLANTATIONS

SINCE NO part of Christopher Codrington's plan had a prospect of fulfillment unless it could be financed, money became a primary concern to the Society : and money, on the Barbadian plantations, was sugar. The board sitting at Charterhouse was concerned with deficits and profits from the money crops. But it must be remembered that, in spite of countless difficulties, they balanced the rights of slaves with the profits from sugar. For at Codrington slave instruction was continued without long lapses, whether or not the account books showed a profit.

Sugar cultivation requires a rich as well as a workable soil, warm air, a plentiful water supply, and good drainage. In these requirements the Society lands were particularly blessed. The elevated location of the upper plantation assured it of excellent drainage, and abundant springs of water, one in particular, which emerged below the cliff where the College came to be placed, proved extremely valuable in dry years and a definite asset to the lower plantation.

The soils on the upper plantation were the Barbadian "reds" as distinguished from the somewhat richer "blacks" of the lower levels to the south and west. The "red" soils, on the whole rather thin, consisted of about 57 per cent of easily workable limestone clay. Under "the Cliff" lay Consetts, its 480 acres grading into the rocky Scotland soils so that the larger section was unfit for cultivation, supporting chiefly forage crops. About one-third of the cane planting was customarily done here. The upper estate consisted of about 270 acres.[1] At the time the Society took over the management of the estates they were said to have comprised about 500 arable acres. For most of the eighteenth century an average of 115 acres produced sugar each year, although it was estimated that at least 150 acres should be the annual average. To attain that average an adequate supply of Negroes was required and necessary herds of cattle maintained. The 258 acres of poor soil were used for grazing or, especially on Consetts, let to tenants.

---

[1] For notes to chap. iv, see pp. 133–136.

Nothing in the Barbados environment played a more important role than the climate. The temperature had its effect on workers and in this respect Codrington was most fortunate. Commonly below 75° F., even in the hottest season, it rarely ascended above 80° in the shade.[3] Rainfall, however, was extremely variable and the annual average of 62.5 inches conveys little meaning in an area where the diurnal, seasonable, and annual variations were so great. Moreover, the easterly trade winds, normally so dependable, at times gave way to hurricanes as in 1731, 1780, and 1831, and these affected not only the crops and buildings of the Society's holdings, but the shipping as well, to the point of calamity.

Sugar cane, which played such a major role in the history of Codrington, as of all Barbados, had been introduced into the West Indies by Columbus himself on his second voyage.[4] Barbados was the first of the British islands to plant sugar cane extensively, that "sweet grass" having been transferred thence from British Guiana or Brazil early in the 1640's. However, it was not until the Dutch, driven out by the returning Portuguese, brought their superior knowledge, industry, and skill to bear on the crop, that the cultivation of sugar cane really gained foothold. Richard Ligon, on his arrival in Barbados in 1647, found the work of sugar making, a new practice there. At the time of his departure, in 1650, the growing of sugar cane was a chief industry of the island.[5] By the early eighteenth century, when the S.P.G. entered the Barbadian scene, the cane had been under cultivation for so long that it was known as "creole," meaning native.

Such were the basic natural and historical factors of the Society's inheritance. About such things the Barbados Committee in London could reasonably expect to be informed. But it is not strange that the various problems of a practical sort, which developed under experimental conditions and were rendered more complex by long-distance management, should have at times seemed insoluble to the English Society which guided the plantation policy. In an attempt to understand sugar economy, members of the Society's Barbados Committee in London, as absentee sugar cane planters, set about gathering information. A handwritten account of the practices of Barbadian planters, dated 1711, is filed with the earliest records of sugar production.[6] From time to time the missionaries and agents in Barbados sent additional material outlining the hazards and difficulties of the sugar business. For example, John Ashley, in 1733, forwarded a pamphlet entitled "The Sugar Trade" with the comment that an understanding of the encumbrances thereon in London would "revive our drooping spirits, and greatly advance the annual balance of Codrington Donation."[7]

In the operation of any sugar cane plantation, the Society learned, three principal factors must be taken into consideration: the lands, the physical equipment, and the stock. For the equipment and maintenance of a plantation of the size held by the Society, a considerable capital was required. A sugar cane planter needed not only more capital than an ordinary English farmer but, said Bryan Edwards, a certain spirit of adventure as well. In fact, lack of adequate capital had begun to eliminate the faint of heart and slim of purse by the time the Society entered the struggle in 1712.[8]

As for equipment, the Society's plantations contained, according to the earliest report, two so-called works, with three windmills and a boiling house and a curing house on one estate, and one windmill, a boiling house, and a curing house on the other.[9] A later report in 1717 speaks for the adequacy of these buildings in commenting that the Codrington plantations had the largest boiling house, the largest still house, and one of the largest curing houses on the island.[10] By July, 1761, almost fifty years later, the buildings on the upper plantation included "two Mills, a Boiling House, Curing House, Mill House, Rum House, Corn House, the Manager's Dwelling and a Stable; all in pretty good order, except the Curing House...." Although the lower plantation was less extensively furnished with buildings, its condition was said to be satisfactory.[11] As for the rest of the plantation equipment, the inventories of goods shipped from England include itemized lists of the various tools required for the making of sugar, molasses, and rum, such as cane crushers, metal and wooden kettles, troughs and evaporating vats, stills, coopering materials, and planting and harvesting tools most important of which were the hoes and machete-like knives called "bills."[12]

Cattle, donkeys, and horses, especially cattle, had to be maintained on the plantation. This livestock was not only used in the work of producing sugar but, more important, the manure was required to fertilize the land. The process of raising sugar cane necessitated extensive artificial fertilization. The soil had at first been enriched by the addition of marl and mold from the gullies which, here and there, furrowed the coralline terraces of Barbados. Later, when large numbers of cattle were imported, to turn the early mills of Barbados, they provided the "major fertilizer." When the windmills displaced cattle mills during the first half of the eighteenth century, the cattle were still kept for their manure.[13] In 1711, John Smalridge wrote, "A Plantation without stock is no more deemed entire here than a Man without hands and feet can be said to be whole; for without Cattle we can't make Sugar, for it is produced by dung and much labor."[14] In spite of the early attempts to maintain soil fertility, the luxurious canes continued to extract their toll and the average yield per acre declined until, in 1779, the Society's attorneys reported that "the land in general in our Country does not now seem to yield its former and natural increase; nor can we resolve this misfortune into anything but the will of God."[15]

One of the earliest methods for spreading fertilizer in early eighteenth-century Barbados is described:

... the practice is to tether cattle to stakes driven into the ground. The spot is covered with good mould, and then well littered with dry and green vegetable matter, which, with the animal manure from the cattle, makes a compost heap sufficient for a certain space of ground. When it is completed the stakes are withdrawn, and placed in another part of the field, in which the same process is renewed, ...[16]

The importance of soil enrichment was, indeed, so generally recognized that James Grainger, a physician turned planter on the island of St. Christopher's, referred to it in a lengthy poem first published in 1764.

> Then, planter, wouldst thou double thine estate?
> Never, ah! never be ashamed to tread
> Thy dung heaps, where the refuse of thy mills
> With all the ashes, all thy coppers yield.[17]

In general, the planting to harvesting period occupied twelve to fifteen months, although various circumstances, usually the weather, might shorten or extend the period. The 1711 account of the methods of Barbadian planters advised that "...planters in Barbados begin to plant the latter end of August and make an End of planting the Latter end of december. Some do sooner and some later and go on to febr. before the planting is over."[18] In later years this practice was somewhat revised, since August planting was considered too early to receive the rains, and late planting required labor which should be engaged in harvesting the preceding crop. In general, September and October were considered the best planting months. For the "cutting of the Canes" the 1711 manuscript states that this began "some tyme about the midle of Jan Some tymes not till feb[r] and turns those Canes into Sugar by the latter End of June. As their Cropps are Large or Small and their Strength of Labour they Conclude their Cropp a month Sooner or Latter."[19]

The repeated references in the letters to London to the need for more slaves for the Codrington plantations take on more meaning with an understanding of the vast amount of labor required in raising a crop of sugar and preparing it for the market. The replacement of Negroes formed no inconsiderable item in the capital expenditure for maintenance and replacement. In fact, with them lay the key, in the opinion of most authorities, to the entire sugar economy. The preparations for planting involved the most arduous toil. The workers were in the fields at sunrise and labored until sundown, except for two hours in the hottest part of the day. The fields were worked by hoe culture, since the soil demanded an even spreading of fertilizer in which the use of the plow did not seem practical.

When planting time arrived, the field hands dug holes at intervals for the reception of the canes. From 40 to 60 Negroes ordinarily holed an acre a day, preparing 3,000 or more holes. The work of hoeing was so wearing, however, that planters sometimes saved their own Negroes by hiring others for this work, paying £8 to £10 per acre. After the holing was completed, the slaves made cuttings from the tops of the canes already growing in another field. As a rule, two cane cuttings laid longitudinally were planted in a hole. The canes were then covered with 2 inches of mold from the excavation. At the end of some two weeks, in which time the young shoots had grown a few inches, slave labor cleared them and more mold was added. This process was continued with careful attention to suckers and the elimination of all weeds until "at the end of four or five months," according to Bryan Edwards, "the banks were wholly levelled and the spaces between the rows carefully hoe-ploughed."[20]

For the harvesting of the canes the Negroes went into the fields with their long, heavy "bills." Cutting was hard work for it had to be done low on the stalk where the cane was toughest. Care had to be taken not to injure the bud from which the ratoon crop would spring, and not to leave too much wood to be cut away later. The skill required for such work on the part of the slaves was responsible for the emphasis on the importance of "seasoned" Negroes. In the fields the canes were reduced to a yard or slightly more in length, loaded on donkey or bullock carts or sometimes, in near-by fields, carried to the mill on the heads of Negroes.

In the milling process less hard labor was required but here, again, specialized jobs called for the more highly trained Negroes. The Codrington plantations were most favorably situated for milling, for here on the windward side of the island, the northeast trades blew their strongest and steadiest during the harvesting months of January to April or May. The wind turned the big windmill sails, or "points," which revolved the upright rollers below into which the canes were fed for crushing. The rollers seized the canes and crushed them twice, entering and returning, extracting the juice which fell into a receptacle below. The crushed canes were then carried to the carts which, drawn by cattle or slaves or both, carried them to the fields where they were spread in the sun to dry. Dried, they were brought back to the boiling house where they furnished fuel for the boiling process.

The extracted juice had, in the meantime, reached the boiling house where it was strained into clarifying pans, eliminating the "cush cush," as the slaves called the waste matter. As early as 1725, John Smalridge reported that he had piped water into the boiling house, which "saves the slaves from a great deal of work in the night."[21] From the clarifiers the liquid entered a succession of three to five copper pots, each somewhat smaller and lower placed than the preceding, which were kept boiling above an open oven into which the fuel was constantly fed.

Night and day the fire must be tended while the pots bubbled, for never was the juice allowed to cool during the reduction to sugar. As the scum rose, Negroes stood by to remove it with a long-handled skimmer so that by the time the last copper was reached, the syrup was practically free from impurities. At the final pot, called a "teach" or "tayche," stood the sugar master, an expert tender who determined when the viscous mass should be removed from the fire as the exact moment of "strike" arrived. The "strike" secured, the contents of the pot were poured into a shallow wood, iron, or copper vat to cool. As it cooled the sugar crystals formed within two or three days. Then the soft, brown mass had to be shoveled either into perforated hogsheads or into pots which were placed in the sugar house on a rack over troughs into which the molasses dripped. After two or three weeks the dripping was completed, the hole in the bottom plugged, and the muscovado was ready for shipment.

Pots were often used for this process at Codrington, since the plantations had their own pot houses and even occasionally made pots for the market. Here, again, the great difficulty was, however, the almost perpetual dearth of labor. In 1748 the attorneys reported that "the Pot House, which is a considerable article in these estates, . . . is now so underhanded, that it turns to no account at all: Whereas pots have been at so good a price this year, that had the work been well supplied, & all our pots sold at the Market price, it would have cleared £500 or £600."[22] The Bishop of St. Asaph, in his recommendations in 1760, again called attention to the "want of Negroes" for the pot house. Properly staffed, he believed it "might employ 30 Negroes & produce at least £350 (Barbadian currency) or £250 (Sterlg.) yearly."[23]

Finally, there was the preparation of rum. Rum was so important a by-product that it sometimes meant the difference between black and red on the balance books. All the skimming and waste from sugar making together with the poorest part of the molasses and the clearings from the clarifiers, were mixed with water into a wash, which then went through a distilling process in the still houses. Taken fresh from the still, the rum was a potent concoction to which the Barbadians early gave the highly appropriate name of "kill-devil." The amount of rum produced annually varied, of course, in proportion to the amount of sugar, the condition of the weather at harvest time, and the market price. When rum sold well, there was less sugar and more rum. The figures varied also because the pots were not always of the same size, although holding usually about 70 pounds; nor did the hogsheads always weigh the same, varying from 13 to 16 cwt.; nor did the same amount of cane juice always produce the same quantity of sugar and rum. In general, Edwards estimated that about 200 gallons of rum were produced with three hogsheads of sugar.[24] A report for Codrington of June 29, 1796, stated, "We have finished our Crop ... 2556 pots [96 hogsheads] of sugar & 6175 gallons of Rum."[25] These figures translate themselves almost exactly into Edwards' proportion.

No year can be cited as typical for the annual sugar output of the Codrington estates. Problems were always present, but the only typical thing about them was their variability and the consequently harrowing undependability of this sugar enterprise upon which the Society had engaged. In a letter of August 28, 1776, the attorneys expressed this continual uncertainty when, writing of the excellent crop prospects, they stated:

... Our Hopes have been so often blighted by some unforseen accidents when there was the fairest Prospect for a good Crop in an ensuing Year, that we had almost determined never again to venture our Opinions ... on that subject but as there is such an ocular demonstration now before us for a very considerable one the next, and ... the estates were never in a more flourishing condition ... it is a Duty which we owe to the Society to transmit ... such Intelligence.[26]

For one thing, there was the effect of the varying weather, and regularly each year a crop report was also a weather report. Drought years were frequent, withering the young canes and reducing the sugar output. When the rains came they sometimes continued to the point of disaster. Thus John Smalridge wrote in July, 1722, that he was unable to break all the canes, "the wet weather coming in and continuing prevent me." Nor could he ship 10 hogsheads of sugar since "I cannot as yet get them down the paths being so bad."[27] By October of 1724 the "perpetual rains for 2 months past" had delayed the ships.[28] And the following year the plantation had "Suffered very much in Loss of Negros in Number, and in Cattle by the extream wett weather, which made me this

Year buy both ... for want of which I can neither plant nor break in June."[29] On the lower estate, the crop "was Ruined what the Rains did not the Grub did."[30]

A period of devastating drought which extended through the early 1730's was followed by excessive rains which much damaged the "Boyling House" on the lower plantation by carrying away the foundation. Then, again, drought descended and, by December 7, 1746, Thomas Rotheram deplored "the melancholy Prospect which the two succeeding Crops afford throughout the whole Island: occasioned by the Dry Seasons which we have lately had."[31] And in the following year John Payne could report "a very miserable poor Cropp.... having no Rain.... We much want a Deep season to put Water in the Ponds & to Wett the Canes to the Roots."[31]

The wind, too, did great damage, especially in hurricane years. When the cane was beaten down by wind along with rain, although it was not ruined, the hardship and costs of harvesting were considerably increased. These storms also played havoc with shipping in the harbor.[32] Additional perils were the pests, the fungus, the grubs, the root borers, the ants, and the rats, all of them with an inordinate desire to feed upon the luscious cane. But the chief complaint was the blast, which was at its worst in dry years. The Rev. Griffith Hughes, whose *Natural History of Barbados* appeared in London in 1750, ascribed the yellow blast, more virulent than a form known as the black blast, to swarms of insects at first invisible, which worked upon the tender blades, impeding the circulation so that the plant withered as if from drought.[33]

There is ample evidence of the effect on the cane. Typical is the account in 1736 of a shipment much less, because of the blast, than formerly produced.[34] In 1747, a drought year, John Payne wrote sadly, "We have the Misfortune to have one Exceeding fine piece of Canes of 14 Acres Intirely Blasted. they were so Bad the Gent. Attorney's advis'd to have them pull'd up & I've replanted them in May last. They seem to look Well. But there is no knowing what to say when the Blast prevails."[35] The carnivorous ants, introduced to help in curtailing the blast, proved an almost greater problem. But just when the planters were at their wits' end, along came the 1780 hurricane and destroyed these pests together, to be sure, with almost everything else.

Such difficulties owing to natural causes were augmented by the problem of transportation. The plantations of the Society lay fourteen miles from the shipping port of Bridgetown, but they had the advantage of Consett's Bay, one of the very few anchorages along the reef-bound coast. The use of a plantation sloop was justified by Mr. Smalridge for its "conveniency to save cattle" the long overland trip to Bridgetown,[36] and the Society usually rented or owned a sloop. In very wet years, especially, the sloop afforded a distinct advantage. A report for 1798, for instance, noting the tediousness of getting a crop away from Consett's Bay, concluded, "[but] we are very lucky upon the whole; for were we to attempt to get away a crop from this part of the Country by land; in the course of one Twelvemonth we should not have a team of Cattle left."[37] When talk of renting the plantations arose in the 'forties, and again in the 'sixties, the advantage of Consett's Bay was also suggested for the additional profits to be derived by the renter who could thus engage in coastwise trading.

After the casks had reached Bridgetown, the agent there saw to their transshipment to ocean-going vessels. Apparently the town agency was rendered attractive by the method of handling the rum. Charles Bolton, in making application for the post in 1732, stated frankly, "the Advantage wch I have is in selling my Own Cask by having the Refusall of the Rum at the Market Price."[38] If rum sold low, the Society, not the agent, suffered. In 1755 there was a good crop but the debt to the town agent, Codrington Carrington, for £1,200 sterling, was due in part to the low price of rum.[39] Rum revenues were offset, moreover, by the necessity of an almost complete rebuilding of the still house on the lower estate in 1754, and by the cost of new stills shipped out from England.

Nevertheless rum was generally supposed to carry much of the operating expense of the plantations, and it often did. As sugar exports increased in the 1790's, the price of rum dropped so that, in 1798, Edward Clarke wrote:

I fancy the Article of Rum will become a drug in this Country before the next crop begins such large quantities of it as has been made. . . . At a meeting of the Planters & Merchants at the beginning of the crop they broke the price of it at 3/6/ Gallon—but at a later meeting of the Merchants they have reduced the price to 3/ & perhaps at some future meeting they might bring it down to 2/6 or 2/ p. gallon. Our Agent Mr. Aylcott will not receive a drop at any price.... He will not take the Rum upon any conditions to give the Plantation credit upon receiving it.[40]

When, as sometimes happened, the manager of the plantation acted also as agent, another opportunity for the manipulation of the rum account presented itself. Again depending upon the price, the manager could vary the amount of rum produced, more rum meaning less sugar. In 1737 an anonymous contributor to the Barbados *Gazette* warned against this possibility. "Observe," he wrote, "he [the manager] did not engage to make any Quantity of Sugar.... And further, no Deficiency in the Sugar is easily chargeable upon him; the Canes were short, they were small, they were dry, they were any Thing; they did not yield; the Liquor boiled away; what would you have, Sir?"[41]

From the Bridgetown docks the hogsheads of sugar were consigned by the agent to different vessels; usually 10 hogsheads per vessel, with the purpose of curtailing losses in event of shipwreck or capture in time of war. For the period 1750 to 1783, largely as a result of almost total losses for every year between 1775 and 1782, except 1780, war played its fateful part in bringing a loss totaling some £8,855 to the Society.[42] In 1746, William Bryant lost much of the equipment for the new college when his ship ran on the rocks.[43] Again in 1759, because of enemy threats, "the Ships went away in such a hurry that great part of the Sugars were unshipped."[44]

Almost always the shipping costs were high. Prices varied during the years 1727 to 1744 from 16s 11¼d to 32s ½d per hundredweight of muscovado. The extreme distance separating Barbados from England required an efficient network of special agents working harmoniously if the sugar crop were to arrive in England within three months after leaving the plantations. Thus it was impossible to anticipate any sudden advance in the sugar price by regulating shipments. Instead, the crop was sent in small assignments to market and stored temporarily to await a favorable sale. En route to London the muscovado sugar had already decreased approximately 10 per cent owing to "Pilferage and Wastage ... and Difference of Tare."[45] The cost of transportation, taxes, and agents' fees multiplied and made an advantageous market a necessity in meeting the growing cost. One of the many invoices for shipment available in the Codrington records is cited as an example. In 1822, 20 hogsheads were sent to England valued at approximately £797. After all the charges were deducted, the S.P.G. received £373. The other £424 went for transportation, customs, insurance, and agents' fees. Thus eleven hogsheads out of twenty were consumed in the process of bringing the sugar to market.[46]

The story of the Society's sugar plantations in Barbados during the first century of their management is, perhaps, best told in the annual accounts of sugar produced and sold. For the most part carefully preserved in the files of the S.P.G., these accounts are especially valuable to the historian since they record the story of a sugar plantation not for a decade only, but for a century. In presenting them, it may be quickly said that the expectation of £2,000 in yearly profit, anticipated in 1711, was rarely attained. Neither was the goal of an annual £3,600 sterling set by the Bishop of St. Asaph in 1760. The Bishop confidently asserted that, with a cane planting of 150 acres, 100 in the upper plantation and 50 in the lower, with each acre producing 1½ hogsheads, an annual yield of 225 hogsheads might be expected. At £12 a hogshead, the crop would gross £2,700 sterling.[47] The expectation of £12 a hogshead was seldom realized; the total acreage seldom reached 150; and 1½ hogsheads could never confidently be expected from each acre. Production varied greatly from year to year, high in some of the early years: 209 hogsheads in 1713; 152 in 1716; 154 in 1723; sinking to 82 in 1739. From 1750 through 1832 the averages for twenty-year periods, as given by Conrad Pile, accountant for the Society, show a gradual increase as they approach the prosperity which began as the nineteenth century opened. Pile's figures are as follows:[48]

Average Annual Clearance for 34 Years from 1750 to 1783...£896   8 2
  do   do   10 Years from 1784 to 1793...1953   6 9½
  do   do   10 Years from 1794 to 1803...1235 17 2
  do   do   10 Years from 1814 to 1823 after
deducting Attorney's Commissions, & during which
period there was an addition of Capital by natural
Increase of Negroes, Horses & Cattle, amounting 3839 18 6 P. Ann.
to £5076.5 which has not been added to the Clearances of the Estate.

In understanding these figures it is important to remember that the different problems which contributed to smaller returns than had been expected were not limited to the Codrington estates. Indeed the crop reports of Codrington parallel closely the reports as given for the whole island of Barbados. The common problems of pests and weather, of tariff and middlemen's profits, of war, and of French inroads on the English sugar trade had, by the middle of the eighteenth century, placed the sugar plantations in Barbados in the hands of a small and select planter class with sufficient capital to withstand the vicissitudes and reap the later profits. Had Christopher Codrington willed his estate to any individual or group less indomitable and resourceful than the S.P.G., it might well have gone the way of so many Barbadian fortunes.

The year-by-year story of the Codrington plantations is told in the reports of crop totals and sugar shipped, the plantation accounts, the careful invoices and receipts included in the records of the Society. For the purposes of this chapter, therefore, an effort has been made to present plantation receipts in the form which will most clearly indicate returns over a considerable period of time with some degree of accuracy. During the early years, up to 1750, when accounting methods varied considerably and reports were only casually forwarded by some of the managers of the estate, the Society's Annual Reports to its members of sugar sold give the best long-term picture. The disadvantage that occasionally total sales for a given year include a few hogsheads left over from the crop of the preceding year, is largely overcome by the long period covered by these reports. The receipts are listed, on page 76, as they appear in the report of the Codrington fund.[49]

A comparison of these figures with the chart prepared by Frank W. Pitman for Barbados sugar for the years 1700 through 1760 demonstrates the representative part played by Codrington in the annual reports of the sugar crop from Barbados. In Pitman's chart the profitable years for the whole island are 1714 through 1718 with totals hovering around £300,000 annually. A slump to below £100,000 in 1721 was recovered by 1724 but, except for good years in 1728 and 1730, the sharp decline had begun. From 1730 until 1760 the total exports exceeded £200,000 in only seven years.[50]

The hard times which began in 1719 were caused in part by the heavy rains reported by John Smalridge, in part by a drop in prices, by distemper among the animals, and by the inroads on the market of sugar grown on the French plantations in Guadeloupe and Haiti, and the more fertile soil of other English islands. The heavy floods of 1724 caused particular damage to the Codrington

Year	Hogsheads	Proceeds	Year	Hogsheads	Proceeds
1712	40	£499.19.00	1733	[no accounts]	
1713	220	3127.10.01	1734	[no accounts but crops	
1714	60	1057.17.03		short in "the whole	
1715	184	3678.15.00		island"]	
1716	180	3185.09.00	1735	[no accounts but crops	
1717	112	1802.11.00		"very short" due to	
1718	90	1444.17.10		blast]	
1719	157	2068.06.11	1736	85	–
1720	90	959.00.05	1737	84	1387.09.09
1721	116	1236.11.10	1738	100	£1597.08.11
1722	50	610.17.11	1739	62	1122.04.03
1723	179	2879.06.01	1740	52	884.14.06
1724	135	2397.11.02	1741	110	1917.10.00
1725	113	£1789.18.11	1742	70	1179.09.019
1726	101	1668.11.11	1743	44	940.14.00
1727	100	1433.09.09	1744	[no accounts]	
1728	98	1642.15.09	1745	68	1428.09.00
1729	138	2255.15.00	1746	35	795.12.11
1730	[no accounts]		1747	60	1480.04.10
1731	93	1422.05.01	1748	74	1371.19.01
1732	93	1235.12.10	1749	50	807.19.11

estates. Parts of the lower plantation situated near the level of the ocean were washed away. Young cane plants had to be bought for the purpose of replanting those sections denuded by the rains, and 525 pounds of yam seeds were purchased for reseeding.[51] Aside from the damage to the sugar crop, the rains caused a delay of two months in the loading of sugar which was difficult to handle in wet weather, and likely to be a total loss if exposed to the rain.[52] There was little shelter for the sugar in transit to market, for whether by cart or by sloop, or lying upon the open wharves, the barrels were exposed to the weather. Moreover, there were transportation difficulties in 1724: cargo vessels were very uncertain.[53] However, later in the summer shipping facilities became more adequate, and the sugar market, as an added compensating factor, was good.[54]

The combination of natural catastrophe with the active inroads of foreign, and especially French, trade during the 1730's was so drastic to Barbadian prosperity that marginal planters left the island in numbers, and the Society apparently decided that it was better not to publish the discouraging accounts of Codrington plantations for its membership. To begin with, there was the destructive hurricane of August 13, 1731, followed by heavy drought in 1733 and 1734. The Molasses Act of 1733 promised some relief from the cost of marketing sugar but it was not seriously enforced. At this time a lively defense of the rights of Barbadians and an accounting of the profits accruing to the Mother Country from the sugar trade began to appear in the Barbados *Gazette*. The colonists advocated direct shipment to foreign markets, as already practiced by the French colonies, and opposed the established British practice of limiting export from the colonies to English markets for reëxport. They warned that "if the Ballance of Trade still continues against us, it will reduce the Island to such Misery as never was yet known here,"[55] and recommended not only "an easier Access to the foreign Markets," but "Some effectual Method to prevent all unnatural Combinations to depreciate the Commodity."[56]

The year 1741 produced a large crop in Barbados which met a declining price in the markets. But crops were irregular; poor crops from 1744 through 1746 decreased the yield, and, with the outbreak of the Seven Years' War, freight rates doubled from 3s. 6d. per cwt. to 7s. 6d., and insurance rates jumped from 7 to 25 per cent.[57]

For the period from 1750 through 1783, a careful accounting gives the picture of Codrington plantations during this time. Titled, "Clearances of the Society's Estates in Barbados from 1750 being the earliest Record of any Accounts to be found, to 1783, in which latter year Mr. Brathwait's Rent commenced," the account is given on page 78.[58]

These figures, marking a period of prosperity from 1755 through 1769, followed by hard times beginning in 1770, are, again, as much a reflection of Barbadian sugar economy for the period as a picture of the Codrington estates. Otis P. Starkey's chart of sugar

Year	Status	Amount		Amount
1750	.	. . .	Sunk	2277. 4. 6¾
1751	Cleared	919.18.6	.	. . .
1752	do	1120.13.6¾	.	. . .
1753	do	1495.16.7	.	. . .
1754	.	. . .	Sunk	542.12. 8¾
1755	Cleared	3081.13. 9	.	. . .
1756	do	556. 4. 6	.	. . .
1757	do	1627.17 1¾	.	. . .
1758	do	2782.13.3¾	.	. . .
1759	do	3052.10.9	.	. . .
1760	do	2744. 2.8¼	.	. . .
1761	do	4214.18.1	.	. . .
1762	do	3705.13.2¼	.	. . .
1763	do	3371. 3.9¾	.	. . .
1764	do	1714.15.	.	. . .
1765	do	990. 2.9	.	. . .
1766	do	2355. 5.5	.	. . .
1767	do	187. 3.10½	.	. . .
1768	do	2317. −.3½	.	. . .
1769	do	2184. 1.10½	.	. . .
1770	do	335.10.2	.	. . .
1771	.	. . .	Sunk	1355. 4. 2½
1772	Cleared	84.18.11¼	.	. . .
1773	.	. . .	Sunk	551.19. 7½
1774	Cleared	53.18.7½	.	. . .
1775	.	. . .	Sunk	1016.10. 3
1776	.	. . .	do	851.14.10½
1777	.	. . .	do	204. 4. 9½
1778	.	. . .	Sunk	249.15. 0¼
1779	.	. . .	do	135.17. 7½
1780	Cleared	378. 9. 6¼	.	. . .
1781	.	. . .	Sunk	899. 2. 2½
1782	.	. . .	do	771.10.11¼
1783	Cleared to Oct. 10	59. 4. 6	.	. . .

39333.16.10

8855.16. 9
30478. . 1

39333.16.10

exports from Barbados to England from 1760 through 1790 shows shipments up to 1770 hovering around 150,000 cwt. But from 1770, a sharp decline began, going down to 50,000 cwt. in 1778. By 1785 the shipments had tripled to 150,000 cwt., from which point they continued to rise.[59]

On the Society's plantations, the reports of good crops began pouring in in 1753, when Thomas Rotheram wrote cheerfully of a harvest "which will considerably exceed that of some years past."[60] Occasionally French ships captured the British cargo vessels and the full crop failed to reach the English market.[61] The important July report to the Society in 1760 rejoiced over the exceptional crops of the past two years. Rum had taken care of all plantation expenses but for the purchase of new Negroes, and the estates were no longer in arrears.[62] But beginning in 1770 the hard times struck with a vengeance. Blasts and ants made inroads on the canes in the 1770's.[63]

With the beginning of the American Revolution not only were London-bound ships the prey of both the French and the Americans, but the New England trade, upon which Barbadians had depended for many of their supplies, was abruptly cut off. Sugar prices jumped 50 per cent between 1775 and 1777, but it was difficult to get the sugar to market. Further, with the lack of imports from the northern colonies, Barbadian sugar planters began to decrease the acreage in canes in favor of subsistence foods. On the Codrington plantations, larger crops of "corn, yambs, potatoes, and plantains," were reported, and such canes as had been planted were infested with borers and suffering from the blast which extended throughout the island.[64] In 1777 there was fear that sugar might have to be sold locally, and supplies "being still withheld from North America almost threatened a famine on other estates on the island." By 1779, with the French fleet at St. Vincent's, blast was taking its toll from what had promised to be a good crop. The final blow was the severe hurricane of 1780, which destroyed not only the sugar crop, but much of the plantation equipment as well.[65]

When Braithwaite rented the plantations in 1783 the low prices of 1783 and 1784 began to rise in the succeeding years. The clear-

ances from October 10, 1783, to October 10, 1793, the period of
Braithwaite's rental, are as follows :[66]

1784	Clear'd	542. 6. 7
1785	do	864.18. 7½
1785	do	1538.11.5 ¾
1787	do	2034. 3.11¾
1788	do	1904.15. 4½
1789	do	1570.14. 1½
1790	do	1399. 4. 3¼
1791	do	2718.18.10½
1792	do	3086. 19. 3
1793	do	3561.15.– ¾

Average annual Clearance of the 10 years is £1953.6.9½ The Society at the end of this period very liberally made Mr. George Barrow a present of £500 for the judicious management of the Estates.

Barbadians in general were prosperous during this period, in
spite of the epidemics of smallpox and yellow fever. Until the
sugar markets lost during the disastrous 'seventies could be recovered, the planters began to grow more cotton, which brought
quicker returns. Sugar prices improved steadily from 1789 to 1793
and were "high" from 1794 to 1799. The introduction of Otaheite
canes from Tahiti, in 1790, later ushered in an era of bumper crops
and reduced the price of sugar.[67]

The ten years under Braithwaite had, once again, cleared the
plantations of debt. When they returned to more direct management by the Society, in 1793, the prosperity was decreased, but an
annual average of £1,235.17.2 for the first ten years, from 1794 to
1803, was maintained. Annual clearances for this decade were as
follows.[68]

1794	Cleared	591.16.10		
1795			Sunk	600.18.00
1796	Clear'd	2186. –. 4¾		
1797	do	1857. 1. 6¼		
1798	do	1738. 2. 2½		
1799	do	1645.13.10¼		
1800	–		Sunk	59. . 5¾
1801	Clear'd	1326.15. 1¾		
1802				
1803	do	3673. . 3		
		13018.10. 2½		659.18. 5¾
				12358.11. 8¾
				13018.10. 2½

The first years following 1794 were profitable ones, for the consequences of the Anglo-French wars had brought rising prices and unstable markets. The destruction of the sugar crop on many of the islands, either by blockade or invasion or by Negro revolts as had occurred in St. Dominque, ushered in a wave of speculation in sugar production unequaled in past experiences. Sugar prices rose from 32s a cwt. to 87s. West Indians expanded their acreages, increased their labor supply, and prepared to reap even greater profits. Captured French islands in the region were hurriedly cleared and planted. The cultivation of cane, however, had pushed ahead of consumption, and the rising prices, which had leaped to such great heights, fell fast.[69]

The Society's plantations did not reap all of the advantages of the favorable market. The new manager, J. Edward Clarke, wrote of good yields in prospect, but the actual receipts of the Society did not register the expected prosperity. The estates did, however, share with other West Indian plantations the effects of inflation. The high prices of provisions and building material, estimated at three times those of former years, ate deeply into the S.P.G. receipts, and Clarke commented in 1797: "It is lucky for us that we made a great many ground provisions upon the Estate or I do not know how I should mannage to feed so many Persons as look up to me for Victuals three times a day. . . ."[70] Moreover, the war brought raids by French vessels upon English convoys and merchantmen.

Beginning in 1804, the plantation clearances were tabulated in relation to the expenses of the reviving college. Entered in ten-year periods, they are given on page 82 for the years 1804 through 1823.[71]

With the marketing of the sugar, the plantation cycle closed, bringing to completion the various processes by which, through the run of season, the green and gold of the canebrakes became converted into funds for the Society's coffers. So difficult was the labor, so great the hazards, so unfamiliar the nature of the occupation and environment, so tenuous the lines of communication, that the survival of the venture was in the nature of a miracle. Perhaps one explanation is that funds were available from the Society aside from the plantation income to tide over the bad years, so that in the long run the school survived where many a less fortunate proprietor was unable to do so. Perhaps the moral force of the humanitarian idea existing in the hearts and minds of a distinguished and determined body of men admitted no thought of possibility of failure on these, God's Sugar Acres.

Plantation Clearances for 10 years		Expenses of Codrington College for 10 years	
1804	1653.11. 7½	1804	1496. 3. 6½
1805	3402.10. 5½	1805	2044. 8. 7¾
1806	921. 2. 9½	1806	1683.12. 8¾
1807	1161. 2. 9	1807	1446. 1.11½
1808	1548.13. 9¼	1808	1035. 7. 1¼
1810	1164.17.10	1809	907.18. 2¾
1811	366.10. 1¼	1810	877. 4. 7
1812	601. 8. 8¼	1811	1330.17. 7¾
1813	266.13. −¼	1812	1173.13.11¼
		1813	1196.10.11½
	11086.11. ½		
1809 Lost this year	44. 8. 8¾		13191.19. 4
	11042. 2. 3¾		

Plantation Clearances for 10 years		Expenses of Codrington College for 10 Years	
1814	3049.10. 2½	1814	1547.10.11½
1815	4963. 9. 3½	1815	1618. 9. 1
1816	7413.19. 3	1816	2273. 6.11½
1817	3980.19. 9½	1817	2142.14. 4½
1818	4700.19. 1¾	1818	1870. . 5¾
1819	5340. 1.10½	1819	3869.10. 2¼
1820	2024. 8. 2½	1820	4353. 9. 2
1821	2555. . ¾	1821	3031. 2. 7¾
1822	2490.10. 8¾	1822	3633. 8.10
1823	3901. 6. 8½	1823	3462.11.11¾
	40420. 5. 3¼		27802. 4. 8

CHAPTER V

Of the Negroes thereon; the Society's establishments for their Instruction; the Obstructions in performing the office of Catechist; the Temper of the Inhabitants; of slow advances against ill-ground Prejudices.

By J. HARRY BENNETT, JR.

THIS CHAPTER sets forth the conflict between an alien idea, that the Negro was a "man and a brother," and the planters' view that he was property. During the eighteenth century in England and France, the one view was called the "cult of the noble savage." The other, that he was property with a savage nature, found its climax in the insurrection and destruction of the greatest sugar island of all, French Haiti, which had furnished cargoes for 1,000 ships, manned by 15,000 sailors. The plantation society of Barbados, aided by its established clergy, was cool toward the Codrington experiment. Could not the endowment be diverted wholly toward the education of whites? Was not Negro education dangerous to the resident planters and their regimes? Instead of a Christian slave and a willing worker, would not the result be African savages quite out of hand?

In fact, it was the split between the idea of the Noble Savage in Paris, and the idea of the planter in Haiti that led to bloodshed in that island. The Society for the Propagation of the Gospel was strong enough to keep its ideal alive but it was unable to make it very effective in practice until the humanitarian crusade at the end of the century forced the planter aristocracy into coöperation. It is interesting that white students shared in the benefits of the legacy. Ignorance, like disease, was detrimental to both races; education beneficial to both.

OF THE NEGROES THEREON

THE STUDY OF slave education at Codrington can be justified on the ground of its accomplishments as a not unimportant part of intellectual history. The Negro schools so painfully developed there during the eighteenth century, helped to establish the Negro's right to a participation in Church society which, particularly in view of the practical, civil importance of that phase of life for the period, was a significant move, to use modern words, toward the breaking down of other white monopolies of privilege.[1] Religious training broadened gradually into a program of general education for the bondsmen. And Codrington Negroes were to take part, eventually, in the carrying of European civilization to members of their own race in Africa and elsewhere.[2]

Most of the period now under consideration is important less for results in Negro education itself than for the interesting picture it presents of the struggle necessary to inject a reform into a society almost united in its opposition or indifference. At Codrington the powerful interests represented by the planters, managers, clergy, and even the Negroes themselves complicated what might otherwise have been a simple story of philanthropy on a Barbados estate and, until the century was almost over, made the tale seem one of social maneuver and frustration, rather than of achievement. Because the proponent of reform, the S.P.G., was very much a part of the established order, working for innovation within and not against this structure, the clashes of interest resulting from the Codrington experiment were dignified. Nonetheless, the basic views of the representatives of Church, State, and economic groups emerge over a single issue in a particular locality. The slow beginnings of the Negro humanitarian program at Codrington are, indeed, as meaningful to social history as are the nineteenth-century successes.

For the greater part of the eighteenth century, the radical factor in the Society's relationship to the Codrington Negroes was not that it possessed them as slaves, but that it proposed to educate them. Into this sphere of West Indian master-slave relationship, where the local clergy had feared or disdained to tread, the Society

---

[1] For notes to chap. v, see pp. 136–140.

made bold entrance. Bishop Fleetwood proclaimed as a goal for the Society, in 1711, that its own slaves were to be Christians, even if no others were: meaning that Negro education at Codrington was to be a part of a general campaign for the conversion of colonial slaves.[3]

There were two reasons then for the Society to extend its Negro program to the West Indies. In the first place, the will of General Christopher Codrington made possible the religious training of Negroes. General Codrington had had unique views for a West Indian aristocrat. He could sympathize with slaves even when they were in rebellion, and he felt that a good worker should be treated as a friend rather than as a slave. Most important, he had pondered the problem of Christianizing the bondsmen.[4] Frank J. Klingberg in his article on "British Humanitarianism at Codrington," states, "Apparently his idea in making the bequest to the Society was that the missionaries, living under monastic rules, could convert the Negroes, give them medical assistance, and raise the level of their abilities as workers."[5] This interpretation of the will was approved by the Society. The Negroes on the Society's estates were to be given religious education by medically trained missionaries, and white children were to be educated at the college for missionary work among the slaves in the British colonies. There were strong forces in Barbados prepared to contest this view that the Negro was intended to be the ultimate beneficiary of the Codrington will.[6]

A second reason for making Codrington a center of S.P.G. missionary activities among the Negroes was the strategic importance to the Anglican Church of the great concentrations of blacks in the West Indies. The Rev. William Johnson reviewed in 1737 the reasons for considering the insular slaves a better field for Christian missionary work than those in the mainland colonies. He found that success in the islands would mean success for the English Church.

... Because the Variety of sectaries in most Parts of the Continent renders it there Impracticable, or at least Less Usefull, for no slaves will be permitted to receive Instruction from Persons of Different Principles, & Consequently the Benefit must be less Extensive, each slave being a Proselyte, to his own master's way of thinking.—Whereas in our Islands the Doctrine of the Church of England alone is Maintained & propagated.[7]

It is well to note here that the S.P.G. leaders thus viewed Codrington as a part of the general scheme of colonial conversion, and not as an end in itself. The missionary looked upon the Codrington experiment as a model, the owners of slaves as a controlled test of a new relationship between master and bondsman.[8] All seem to have agreed that the results there would have extended practical effects. "The eyes of all are upon the College," said the Rev. Arthur Holt in 1727, "as they are inquisitive what steps are taken for the Conversion of those Slaves, as if good or bad success there, must be an Index for the whole Island."[9]

With so much at stake, the Society launched its project with some care. The Rev. Joseph Holt, recommended by the Bishop of London for the post of catechist to the Codrington Negroes, was found "very fit and qualified," after an examination of his testimonials from various heads of the University of Cambridge and from several London physicians. Holt, formerly licensed for North America, was to be paid a salary of £100 sterling a year, in addition to receiving board and lodging at the Society's plantation house for himself and wife.[10] He was required to prove his skill in caring for the sick, doubtless an acknowledgment by the Society that General Codrington had had the Negroes in mind when he specified that men trained in "physick and Chirurgery be obtained."

In considering the above facts, it is well to associate with them certain other matters that determined the S.P.G. policies. No stigma was attached to slaveholding, even by churchmen. The Society directed affairs from across the ocean, and operated through local men, who were certain to apply the prevailing practices of Barbados, including those based on the view that it was cheaper to buy slaves than to conserve supplies by good treatment.[11] A college was built and supported by the labor of Negroes. It proved difficult to make the slave both a beneficiary and a source of profit. But if, during the century, the Codrington establishment was only a slender thread in a program of Negro conversion, it must be recognized that on most West Indian establishments there was no thread at all. A further fact of significance is the listing, in a government report for 1812, of Codrington as the solitary school for Negroes in the whole West Indian world, excepting only the school of the Christian Faith Society in Trinidad.[12]

From time to time, the Society attempted to obtain laws to force planters to permit and pay for the religious instruction of slaves, but without success.[13] Bishop Fleetwood and other S.P.G. leaders were convinced that "the most effectual Way to convert the Negroes, was by engaging their Masters, to countenance and promote their Conversion."[14] Codrington was to be so administered as to prove to masters that the religious program was not expensive, and that it did not lessen the laboring utility of the slaves. Codrington had to compromise the ideal practice with planter prejudices and interests. It was necessary that the work of Negro conversion should proceed successfully in an otherwise normal plantation situation.

The plan which the Society hoped would overcome planter opposition and meet the requirements for expansion throughout the West Indies, was the system of catechists, low-paid specialized teachers, who could move freely from plantation to plantation, consult the masters on free hours, and also offset the prejudices of the local clergy by a vague acknowledgment of their power of supervision. Nor were the Negroes excluded from this type of within-bounds instruction. In 1740 the Society recommended that their project in Charleston, South Carolina, for the training of Negro teachers, be extended to the Codrington estates with the purpose of increasing the opportunities for instruction by utilizing Negro leaders.[15] A draft of the catechist plan "for forcing the baptism and religious instruction of Negroes," specified that catechists were to be provided for the African factories, Barbados, Jamaica, and other slave possessions. Attendance of Negroes upon the teachers was to be forced by the planters, who were to pay a certain sum per capita for each of their slaves. Governors were to seize the slaves of masters who failed to conform to the law.[16] Another, but voluntary, scheme was proposed by the Rev. William Johnson, who suggested that a catechist be placed in each of the three chief towns of Barbados, Antigua, and St. Christopher.[17]

Codrington, however, the source of proof and inspiration, was meeting as the S.P.G. reported, with "impediments."[18] The Rev. Joseph Holt had to be discharged within a few months of his appointment. Of the various charges sent against him by unidentified Barbadians, the Society chose desertion as the reason for dropping him from their rolls. Whether or not prejudice against his program may have influenced the letters of protest,[19] it is clear, at least, that Holt did make an unauthorized trip to North America, "where his stay beyond his Intention was Necessitated by a severe sickness which returned him a very weakly person. . . ."[20] The Rev. Charles Irvine, who served as temporary catechist until another Englishman could reach Barbados, was charged by the parish minister with having been on the estates for catechetical work only twice during his term.[21] The worst that could be said, it seems, of his successor, the Rev. William Brown, was that he died in less than a year after his arrival.[22] After a short period of service by a Rev. Charles Love, the discouraged Society left its slaves more or less spiritually unattended from 1717 to 1726.[23]

These early years reveal the difficult problems that arose from personnel. So much depended upon the man chosen to operate in the edges of the Empire, and there seemed no adequate test for physical and moral stamina short of trial in the field. Most of the catechists came fresh from England, each in turn usually possessed with a sincere enthusiasm to reap slave souls, but quite unprepared to find such completely unworked ground. Disillusion must have been quick and severe for any who could express wonder, as did Thomas Wilkie, that his charges "were altogether ignorant of Adams transgression, and Gods infinite mercy in sending Jesus Christ the second person of the Blessed Trinity to Redeem lost mankind. . . ."[24] If the slaves had somehow failed to discover the doctrines of sin, infinity, the Trinity, redemption, and mediation during their opportunities as field hands, the teachers were generally no less ignorant of the Negro dialects and the idiom best used in instructing the blacks. A teacher from England could so learn to adapt his speech only after several years, according to one experienced missionary.[25]

A roll call of the catechists who served at Codrington shows "the toll taken" by illness and death, together with the persistent efforts of the Society to furnish replacements. As has been seen, of the four catechists between 1713 and 1717, one deserted and one died. Thomas Wilkie, who acted from 1726 to 1733, died insane, and was succeeded by Sampson Smirk. The Rev. Joseph Bewsher began his work in 1745 and resigned in 1750 because of ill-health. The Rev. John Rotheram, who followed Bewsher, was succeeded by the Rev. Thomas Falcon in 1753, Rotheram having been promoted to master of the school. Falcon in his turn became master in 1759, and the Rev. John Hodgson took the position of catechist, dying in 1762. The Rev. Thomas Duke pleaded ill-health after a very short time, and David Davies resigned rather than take clerical orders. The Rev. Thomas Wharton followed Davies in 1766, but resigned because of ill-health in 1768. There were thus thirteen different catechists and many years of interrupted activity during the first half century of Codrington's attempts to win over the Negroes to Christianity.[26]

It will be noticed that six of these catechists either died in office or resigned because of ill-health. Possibly some of those who left Codrington's service on the ground of ill-health were moved to some extent by the comparatively meager salary. The allowance was placed at £100 sterling for Holt and £150 for his successor, with allowance for free board and lodging.[27] But Smirk was allowed but £80 Barbados currency, partly because Arthur Holt thought it better to keep catechists on confining pay.[28] The Rev. William Johnson agreed to the terms made for Smirk, but wrote the Society, "If he proceeds to instruct the Negroes with the Same care & dilligence as hitherto, I humbly conceive he deserves better Encouragement, 80£ P. ann. being but bare subsistence."[29] It was perhaps natural that Smirk, a layman of indifferent education, should have been underpaid, but the salary of the Rev. Joseph Bewsher and his successors, who served not only as catechists, but also as ushers of the college, was only £70 sterling. In 1766 the attorneys attempted to increase the pay of the Rev. Thomas Wharton to £100 sterling, a sum which a grammar school had been paying him for twelve years. The Society did not grant an addition, and Wharton soon found himself in ill-health.[30]

There was a tendency for the island authorities to consider the Codrington men a convenient reserve for vacant parish posts. Governor Henry Worsley, who took the Codrington experiment in Negro education more seriously than many, regretted that the Society employed a lay catechist. "I am persuaded," he wrote, "it would be very much for the advantage of the church here, if the Society . . . would keep a Clergyman at their Colledge here to teach, & Cathechise the Negroes, who would be ready at any time to supply a Vacancy instead of the Schoolmaster they keep there now . . ."[31] Of course, this was what the S.P.G., for the integrity of its own organization, was attempting to avoid. The instructions to the Rev. Mr. Brown, for example, emphasized that he must not accept a benefice if he wanted to retain his college position.[32]

The attraction of the benefices open to Codrington missionaries sometimes involved them in island politics. The Rev. James Butcher, headmaster of the school and occasionally the catechist, held the parish of St. John's temporarily in 1770, until Governor William Spry could appoint his brother, the Rev. Benjamin Spry, to the position. Later, Michael Mashart, a catechist, administered the parish for the absent rector. The plurality of office holding was discovered by the Society in 1774, and both Mashart and Butcher were discharged.[33]

This involvement of S.P.G. missionaries in the clerical politics of Barbados, at a time when there was no essential line of division there between lay and Church matters, is of high significance in explaining the slow development of Negro education at Codrington. Negro reform, spiritual or otherwise, was an imported idea. It was a concept which depended for its strength on the churchmen in England who, away from the West Indian scene of whites outnumbered by Negroes in a planter-dominated society, could with theoretical detachment see slaves only as a rich field for the expansion of Anglican Christianity.

During this period the letters of the catechists to the Society were concerned more with their problems than with the details of the teaching program. Thomas Wilkie, 1727, had taught five or six Negro youngsters to "spell very prettily and repeat the Creed and Lords prayer. . . ." He had three adults under regular instruction, and two of these he had persuaded to attend the Sunday church services. These two could "repeat the Creed & Ten Commandments & Lords prayer almost perfectly. . . ." The three slaves had agreed to take "one wife a piece, forbare working on Sundays . . . an[d] live conformably to the Laws of the Gospel to the best of their knowledge. . . . The more they are instructed they become more desirous to learn, and seem much concern'd what will become of their immortal souls," Wilkie observed. He had taught them to read. One of his pupils belonged to a neighboring plantation.[34]

We may wonder that Wilkie, with several hundred Society Negroes assigned to his care, should have been instructing with any regularity only seven or eight of these slaves, and that he could be looking to neighboring plantations. The explanation was simple. Only with the greatest difficulty had he been able to find a place for his work in the plantation routine. It was necessary that he capture as well as teach the slaves. Of the children he reported:

> The younger I find very docile & capable to learn any thing but that so soon as they are capable of doing they are imployed in looking after the Cattle & Stock so that they have but very little time to learn in and they are very unwilling to come near me and many times when they see me run away and hide themselves among the bushes from me. . . .[35]

If the manager would but command the children to come to him for an hour a day, Wilkie thought, he could in a few years teach them the principles of religion, as well as reading.[36] When this letter reached London, a sharp order went out to Smalridge, informing him that the Society had "very much at heart" the work of the catechist, "and . . . they do require you to give your best assistance to promote this work."[37]

On no point was the Society more consistently emphatic than on that of providing time for the slaves to attend compulsory instruction. In 1713 orders had gone out that the slaves were to be allowed to work for themselves on Saturday afternoons, so that they might have nothing to do but attend upon the catechist on the Sabbath day.[38] The managers were reminded of this regulation from time to time. In 1728 the order was renewed, but it had to be repeated in the next year in a very blunt and stern letter.[39] Shortly after this, the manager, John Smalridge, informed the attorneys that the slaves must be given free time on Saturday afternoons, "except on some Extraordinary Occasion in the Crop Time," as though this were a new procedure.[40]

During the term of Smirk as catechist (1733–1744), the ideal of teaching the children on weekdays and the adults on Sundays seems to have been established.[41] Attendance on instruction was still voluntary in practice, however, which meant that only a few of the slaves were actually instructed. Manager Abel Alleyne interpreted his instructions to mean that baptized blacks were to attend Smirk, but not the more numerous heathen, and during crop time the slaves had no special time for themselves, which caused them to ignore the catechist on Sundays.[42]

Patiently the Society informed the management that it had been intended that no slave should be exempt from the teaching program.[43] For a time after the opening of the college in 1745, the children received an hour and a half of morning instruction each day, and the adults seem generally to have attended Sunday services.[44] With this pattern of revived and ignored orders, we must not be surprised to find, even as late as 1819, that another catechist, the Rev. John Pinder, was pleased that the manager had agreed to give the slaves free Saturday afternoons and Sundays outside of crop time.[45] As Bishop Beilby Porteus noted in 1783, the S.P.G. gave good directions, but it was doubtful that "these directions have always been punctually complied with in the degree and to the extent proposed . . ."[46]

The chief opposition lay, of course, in the whole mood of the planter society which was inclined to regard the S.P.G. Negro program "as a piece of Religious Knight Erranty."[47] There were many accusations that the Barbados planters were irreligious,[48] but men sensitive to their dependence upon one of the most important of all eighthteenth-century economic institutions, the West Indian sugar plantation, and upon slave labor as their greatest single capital investment, did not view the S.P.G. plan at Codrington as a purely religious question. The proposal that slaves should be baptized and instructed for that purpose meant that the Society, which hoped to back its successful example by law, was attempting to apply locally its policy that the property right of the planters was limited by the right of the slaves to at least the minimum of education required for membership in the Church. They would thus become persons rather than property.

Not only did this threaten to upset the usual manner of treating the bondsman, but it held the immediate possibility of depriving the planter of a portion of slave labor time, a commodity for which the masters had more lucrative purposes. The planters probably disliked the idea of having representatives of the Church present on their estates for purposes of instruction, feared that they would have to support the program of the Church out of their own pockets, and suspected the loss of caste should their slaves become Christians. We know that they did balk at the Church attempt to reserve at least Sundays for the indoctrination of the Negroes. If Sundays were given up to religion, other days would have to be allowed the Negro to permit him to provide or to supplement his food provisions.[49]

For many years the planters used as their chief argument against Negro conversion their supposed fear that a baptized slave would thereby be rendered free.[50] It seems clear that the Rev. William Johnson, a Codrington attorney, was correct in assigning the fear of slave labor loss as a more weighty, although seldom mentioned, cause of opposition to Codrington and to Negro education:

> ... I have too great reason to believe that there are very few masters here that would on any Christian consideration give up so much of their Negroes' time from their labors as would be necessary for their instruction, and until they have more pure disinterested hearts, they will be a constant obstruction to the Society's expectation from the intended Charity.[51]

The S.P.G. leaders usually denied that masters would in any way suffer by the Christianization of slaves, but their agents at Codrington gave offhand evidence of the actual economic loss to the planter. The Rev. Joseph Bewsher, in 1745 for example, opposed renting the Codrington plantations, for he doubted that any other manager would permit the education of Negroes: "For supposing that he agrees to their being catechized at the usual Times, (which is a Thing scarce to be expected); I make no doubt but he will endeavour to discourage it upon all Occasions; since it will interfere very much with his own Interest."[52] Others emphasized that not even the little Negroes could be spared for weekday instruction.[53]

> We have a great Number of them at the College every Sunday on the Afternoon, & particularly the Christians, where they are catechised according to the Directions of the Society. They behave in a very decent and becoming Manner at the Time of divine Service, & not less so when they repeat the Catechism. Thirty young Negroes are catechised every Morning at the College ... fourteen of which are those which were bought into the Plantation betwixt two & three Years ago. They cou'd at my Arrival repeat the Lord's Prayer, the Apostle's Creed & the two first Commandments & can now repeat all the Commandments very distinctly & plain. The Others were born in the Plantation, & can repeat the whole Catechism.[54]

Bewsher had, for the time being, established Negro education as a routine program reaching a fair proportion of the slaves but, unlike Wilkie, he was relying on purely oral methods of instruction. The usual S.P.G. policy with respect to the heathen had been to "excite in them an earnest Desire to read the Bible."[55] On the Society's own plantations, however, there was at times great difficulty in enforcing this program. Abel Alleyne protested that it could not be done "from the little time allow'd them," and Bewsher was inclined to follow his policy.[56] But he did seek approval from London to teach the very small children the alphabet.[57]

It is difficult, because of the personnel factor which was a part of every teaching situation, to assess the whole program for Negroes during these years. At times as many as one-third of the blacks were nominally Christians.[58] But in 1745 Bewsher was discouraged at the results of the work under progress at Codrington, believing there had been only "bad progress."[59] Throughout the century the S.P.G. urged that "only beginnings" had been made, and on the plantation, the officials agreed on the "impracticability of instilling into Negroes the principles of religious knowledge."[60] Actually the problem of Negro instruction was the responsibility of a whole society. Only large social changes were eventually to salvage the idea of Negro education from the ruinous futility to which Barbados planters had reduced it by direct influence upon the Codrington program and indirect modification of S.P.G. policy.

The teaching of reading, it must be remembered, was not only a major gain for the slave, but it greatly increased the time required for slave education. Although the Society consistently urged that learning to read was a part of becoming a Christian, the men on the scene in Barbados sometimes reflected community pressure in this respect. In 1737, the Rev. William Johnson pointed out that religious training, "without attempting to teach them to read or write," would "at once answer the same good End proposed . . . & in some measure remove Peoples Prejudices."[61] The explanatory letter of the Rev. Thomas Wharton, the catechist who had never catechized a slave in his term of office, illustrated further the difficulty of maintaining an ideal away from the English environment that had formed it. Wharton defended the standards of slavery as superior to the conditions of the European peasantry, held that there was no time to educate blacks, for "the smallest Negroes as soon as they are able to speak are in some Measure found useful," and ended by arguing that General Codrington, in his will, had meant that slaves were to be used to support white education when he said that they were to be "kept" on the estates.[62]

On the other hand, there were men of untiring devotion, who were delighted with the eagerness of the Negroes in learning to read, and wrote enthusistically to London of the progress to be expected if a concentrated program could be maintained. Such a person was J. H. Pinder, catechist on the estates from 1819 to 1826. A native Barbadian, Pinder took a strong stand in favor of Negro education as "in every way coincident with the colonial interest ... while it effectually secures progressive amelioration in the disposition, understanding, and habits of the slaves." Codrington, Pinder believed, had a special trust to "afford a Model for other Proprietors to follow—And most ardently may this event be expected, when it is seen in what harmony Religious Institutions and Flourishing Agriculture subsist."[63]

A further attempt of the planters to reduce the importance of Codrington as a center of Negro education took the form of an insistence that Christopher Codrington's benefaction had been only for the purpose of providing a school for the general education of the whites. This view disregarded the facts that the General had had the religious instruction of Negroes as his major objective and that the only justification for white education was to train missionaries to the non-European peoples of the colonies. During the first few years of the Society's ownership of the estates, some of the most important figures in Barbados society had assisted in the advancement of the college, but in thanking the Society for its "Generosity ... in applying the whole Donation to this use ..." they clearly hoped to establish that the entire charity would be used for the education of West Indian whites.[64] Relations with these men became more and more strained as the Negro education continued and nothing was done to admit white students to the schoolhouse. Governor Lowther and others assumed a misappropriation of funds.[65] Charles Cunningham, a Barbados minister, perpetually in opposition to the conduct of affairs at Codrington, seemingly dismissed the charity rendered to the slaves when he charged that it was time the Society did something for the poor.[66] In 1729 Arthur

Holt thought some of the sentiment against the college might be removed if the Society would admit the children of white Barbadians to the institution.[67]

When the whites were admitted to the school in 1745, there was no immediate reduction of attention to the Negroes, although the catechist now also served as usher to the school. But this work gradually declined with the decline of the college and, by 1760, the Rev. John Hodgson replied to a Society inquiry with a statement concerning the obstructions to teaching the Negroes, and added that only the slaves on the domestic staff were receiving religious instruction. The Society expressed its regret that these barriers existed but, as always, urged that the work be pushed.[68]

In 1768, when another catechist, the Rev. Thomas Wharton, resigned, the Society again requested information concerning the program of Negro conversion.[69] The schoolmaster, the Rev. James Butcher, replied that since the time of Hodgson's letter of 1760, the entire program of Negro instruction had been abandoned. The London office, which had been publicly calling attention to the work with the Negroes, received this message with what must have been no little surprise. Butcher attempted to vindicate himself, saying that he would attend to the Negroes on Saturdays, but he could not spare time on Sundays, for he must officiate at a chapel service for the whites.[70] Quite clearly, Codrington was not always in the hands of men dedicated to the cause of the Negroes.

The Society's sincere desire to support Negro education was shown in 1775 when it closed the college in the face of financial difficulties, but continued the office of catechist to the Negroes.[71] The Rev. Michael Mashart, given charge of the program, had been brought to London for clerical orders, and thoroughly impressed with the preëminence of the goal of Negro education at Codrington.[72] In addition to the catechetical program, the Society suggested that the slaves be instructed in reading and mathematics. The attorneys were horrified. "With respect to the Instruction of the Negroes in the Principles of Religion and Mathematics," they wrote, "we are sorry that we are obliged to differ in opinion from the Society, being fully convinced that such a Plan will never either answer the Intention of the Benefactor, nor the wished for Desires of the Society."[73]

Thus the attorneys subscribed to the opinion expressed by Thomas Wharton which, in the view of this writer, summarizes the planter's attitude:

> The Time I trust will come when Persons of all Complexions will embrace one Hope, and one Faith, but I am persuaded that that Period is not yet arrived, and in vain will it be to attempt inculcating the purest & most perfect System of Religion, without first implanting amongst them the Principles of civil Government and social Life: And such a Government, I may venture to affirm, the Policy of this Colony will never admit of.[74]

In brief, religion demanded education, and education and slavery as it was constituted, were incompatible.

If space permitted, it would be possible to cite many instances of how the unfriendly atmosphere of Barbados had repressed the Negro project at Codrington less directly than through influence on the attorneys and catechists. Negroes were ridiculed for their forced attendance at services while others were going to market or visiting.[75] Ministers feared legal action should they help to convert Codrington slaves.[76] In general, the local parish clergymen remained cool toward the Codrington work. In 1788, for example, they gave half-hearted support to the idea of Negro education as a principle, but stated, "As for the Clergy, they will find sufficient employment in maintaining their station, and in defending the established faith from the inroads of scepticism and irreligion, the genuine offspring of vice and immortality [*sic*]."[77] It is well to remember that these clergymen were dependent upon local interests, and that they were, as we have seen, closely tied to colonial politics. Like pressure exerted on the press also kept that force from advocating Negro conversion. A publisher, Abel Clinckett, explained in a letter in 1827, that he had omitted religious pieces from his newspaper from "the apprehension that my subscribers would say, I tired them out with Religion and Slave instruction." He continued:

> Many an edifying & beautiful passage have I marked for publication, I have afterwards put it aside, from the fear of exciting injurious feelings against me, & thus counteracting my anxious endeavours to lighten my load of debt, & procure comforts for my family, nearly forty of whom, including slaves, are dependent on my feeble exertions.... Oh! how I should despise the narrow prejudices & the illiberal threats of the public, if I were as independent in purse as I am and ever have been in mind.[78]

Having intended in this chapter to show the significance of the program of Negro education as an idea in conflict with Barbados society, the successful fruition of the Codrington experiment after 1797 can only briefly be indicated here. The Society, more and more under the influence of humanitarian ideas leading toward abolition, became less solicitous of advancing only in accordance with the expressed prejudices of the masters. It proclaimed reading as an absolute essential to Negro conversion, and the curriculum at Codrington was broadened with classes in reading and sewing.[79]

Even more important, the general standards for treating the Negroes were raised. The managers of the S.P.G. estates, who had tended to discourage such improvements, believing a large crop to be the only real recommendation of their services, were made strictly accountable to attorneys sympathetic to the Society's ideals. The slaves themselves, who had resisted Christianity when it gave them no advantages, but rather interfered with their habits of plural marriage, Sunday marketing, and their own religious beliefs, now became much more coöperative when the missionaries offered the benefits of civilization along with Christianity.[80] In this way an expanded and positive program for Codrington Negroes began to furnish practical demonstration to masters in Barbados of the spiritual and pecuniary advantages of improvement in slave life and education. In 1799 Edward Clarke, manager of the Codrington estates, summed up this new state of affairs when he wrote that "few Negroes in the island behave better than those upon the Society's Estates," and that few had better treatment, for "they have every indulgence and encouragement that Negroes can have and I believe they are sensible of it."[81]

The program for improving the lot of the Negro at Codrington was broad in its scope. In addition to the opportunities to learn to read and write, and the courses in mathematics, there was increased concern for the physical health and comfort of "the Society's family." At the turn of the century, the plantation manager, Edward Clarke, reported that "in sickness they have every care and attention paid them; an Apothecary that understands his business, Medicine and everything else that is proper, and in cases of need either Surgeon or Physician called in." One motive for this enlightened health program is revealed by Clarke's further comment as stemming from the growing threat of the abolition of the slave trade and the resulting concern for the well-being of the Negroes in hand. For, pointing to his various efforts to improve the conditions for his Negroes, he added in bewilderwent, "with all that I cannot get them to Increase."[82]

In 1824 a program for better housing was instituted with plans for "the new Negro village" taking shape.[83] These houses were built of stone, with shingle roofs, and each one was provided with a garden, and trees were planted to increase the beauty and comfort of the surroundings.[84] The Barbados committee, in London, approving of these plans, suggested that these new homes might serve a double purpose by encouraging the marriage of slaves. It should be noted here that, after 1819, the Society and its representatives in Barbados had, usually against the opposition of the planters, insisted upon marriage for slave couples as a civilizing influence and, more particularly, as a means of discouraging adultery.[85] With the housing project well under way, therefore, the Committee recommended "that such further inducements as a superior habitation, and additional comforts of clothing, and security of the customary inheritance to their legitimate children ... and any other privileges be offered," to encourage Christian marriage.[86] It is interesting to note in passing that the poor whites on the island often shared in these improvements in the status of the slaves. Bishop William Hart Coleridge was interested in projects in Antigua and Barbados which offered a free meal daily to "the poor free people, both white and colored,"[87] and at Codrington the new chapel under construction for the Society's "Tenantry" was designed to serve "as well ... a very thickly peopled neighborhood of free coloured people."[88]

Several factors were important in making these improvements possible. Codrington could not have supported as expensive a program as it did in the nineteenth century without its improved financial condition. It would be a mistake, however, to ascribe the advance to a mere surplus of funds. A chief determinant toward the success of Negro education at Codrington was a gradual change in Society policy, as revealed most markedly in the Annual Sermons. The essence of this policy at the beginning of the eighteenth century was a contract idea that the master could have his slave unchanged in status in this world in return for making possible the Negro's reward in heaven. Bishop Edward Chandler, in 1719, thus pointed out that the planters were spiritually in debt to the Negroes for the temporal advantages they derived from slavery.[89] The burden of slavery might even be a spiritual advantage to the slaves, Bishop William Fleetwood suggested in 1711, adding that it was better to be sold as a slave than to die in sin.[90] If there were hardships, the planter should "alleviate that Distress, by furnishing their Minds with good Principles," as Bishop Isaac Maddox put it in 1734.[91] But gradually this point of view was revised. Bishop Thomas Secker observed in 1741 that the slaves could only regard the missionary as a representative of the interests exploiting them, and it was impossible to give Christianity any meaning for them as long as their lives remained otherwise unchanged.[92] If we take the speech of Bishop Beilby Porteus, in 1783, as a turning point in the Society policy, agreeing with him that civilization of the Negro had to precede Christianization, we can mark the inevitable time lag between the new ideals and the real beginning of successful education at Codrington.[93]

The evolving attitude of the Society was only part of a general social movement. If humanitarian trends had touched the S.P.G. alone, Codrington might have been a successful center for slave uplift, but it would have been an isolated model. The spread of humanitarian ideals, which was eventually to lead to the emancipation of the slaves, forced the planters in Barbados to follow not too far behind Codrington. The blockades of the late eighteenth-century wars, the opening of an effective parliamentary attack on the slave trade in 1787, and the provisional acts of parliament regulating the slave trade warned planters gradually that they not only needed moral prestige to stave off abolition, but that they must prepare to depend upon their own slaves to breed future requirements. This program necessarily meant that the slaves must be better treated if they were to reproduce.

The planters did raise standards until the island that had felt it necessary to import thousands of slaves each year in order to maintain the Negro population, found itself quite independent of the African trade.[94] Once shorter working hours, lighter discipline, and other advantages to the slave became an economic virtue, the attitude of the planters toward Negro education became so benevolent as to seem almost incredible to a student of an earlier period. Bishop Porteus noted in 1783 that planters ceased to fight slave education when "induced to treat their slaves, especially the females and their children, with more than ordinary tenderness and indulgence, in order to supply their want of Negroes by their own natural population."[95] In 1829, the Bishop of Barbados could report that the governor and his staff had sat down to "good English Plum puddings" with 300 free and slave Negroes, who had been examined in reading, writing, ciphering, and needlework.[96] Planter contentions about the inability of the slave to learn, the possibility that he would revolt if taught, and many other objections disappeared when the masters were forced to undertake the improvements which they had feared Negro education would entail.

If the Codrington plantations had not always come up to the expectations and commands of the Society in its program for the education of its slaves, they represented a single instance in Barbados where a program of education had been insisted upon for the greater part of a century. Further, methods of Negro instruction, tested and perfected by Codrington catechists, were available when the planter society at length accepted a program of amelioration under threat of emancipation measures. In this connection, the influence of the mobilization of opinion on the British home front on the issue of slavery can be noted in the Society's records. When, on January 21, 1831, the Codrington trust announced its purpose to accelerate the complete emancipation of the slaves on the Barbados estates, the Rev. Thomas Guyth, for the Bodwin District Committee of the S.P.G., wrote that the report was "decidedly beneficial to the Society's Interests. It has confirmed several who were wavering, removed misapprehension in some, and allayed uneasiness in others."[97]

The fact that the Barbadian managers of the Codrington estates could accept emancipation, when it arrived by government edict, without "quite so much gloom and despair" as was shown by most of the planters is significant. On July 28, 1834, Forster Clarke wrote the Bishop of Barbados that he had talked with his slaves at Codrington, who were naturally excited, but who "loudly and without exception" declared "their gratitude to me and acknowledging the efforts which I have long ago made for their improvement and the amelioration of their condition."[98] A century of purpose, however sporadic its results at times, had worked to produce a pattern for working out the new problems of apprenticeship and complete emancipation. The opposition of Barbadians to the Codrington movement and to Negro education had begun to disappear and the Society was then free to take advantage of new economic resources in leading the masters in advances that looked toward making slaves, in the words of Bishop Beilby Porteus, not "*nominal*, but *real* Christians."[99]

CHAPTER VI

Of the State and Advancement of the College for the whole West Indian world; the Manner and Time of Instruction; the Particulars of the Constitution; the maintenance of a Convenient number of Professors and Scholars; and the Society's concern that the good General's wisely calculated Charity take full effect.

By JEAN BULLEN and HELEN LIVINGSTON

THIS CHAPTER, too, is a study of an adaptation of English personnel to a tropical climate, a slave regime, and a community which was, on the whole, more concerned with immediate economic gain than with the longer-range problems of cultural development. The colonials were, as remarked above, often resentful over the usurpation of their economic or political rights by the home government. But in the field of education and culture they were less jealous of the rights of the colonies and more inclined to rely wholly on English institutions.

In founding continental colleges—William and Mary in 1696, Yale in 1701,—the white populations could in time furnish the faculty, students, and funds. But in the West Indies, leading men sent their children to be educated in England, and thus local funds were drained away.

OF THE STATE AND ADVANCEMENT
OF THE COLLEGE

IMPLICIT IN THE idea of the college outlined in the will of Christopher Codrington according to patriotic Barbadians was the recognition that the West Indian world must learn to meet the problems of white settlement in the tropics by retaining a portion of the best men and wealth within the colonies. A plantation economy, geographical situation, and a population base of cavalier refugees had produced in Barbados in the eighteenth century a society of rich planters, poor whites, white servants, free Negroes, and slaves. The sharp caste lines drawn by such a social system yielded the advantage of education only to those young sons of wealthy planters who could go to England, or for whom private tutors could be imported. Commenting on this state of affairs, a "person of considerable quality who has lived in Barbados" wrote the Bishop of London early in the century that the young men from the Barbados estates being in England for study at twelve years of age "soe farr removed from their Parents Inspection scarcely one of them is ever knowns not to return utterly debauched both in Principles and Morralls."[1]

The slave economy likewise tended to exclude the poorer whites from even elementary training in skills and handicrafts. It will be recalled that the Society was forced to send carpenters and joiners from England in order to complete the college buildings, a commentary on the shortage of skilled white labor which was a by-product of a slave system. Codrington's bequest, therefore, seemed to many to offer the opportunity not only to furnish education in Barbados for the planter families but, with its provision for foundation scholars, to give to worthy sons of the less fortunate some training in the skills of trade or in the tools of culture up to the limit of their "ability."

From the beginning the plan and program of the school sought not only to fulfill its missionary objective but also to give to Barbadians an education after "the established schools in England," a phrase which appears repeatedly in the records. But English education was itself in a state of transition between the classicism

[1] For notes to chap. vi, see pp. 140–144.

of an earlier century and the growing demands of a practical age concerned chiefly with commerce and empire. The younger sons of the landed gentry were not above being "bound apprentice" to the trades, thus combining their inherited prerogatives with the profits of trade and empire.[2] At Christ's Hospital, the grammar school furnished instruction, clothing, maintenance, and lodging to children from seven to fifteen years of age, serving both as a grammar school for the indigent and as a stepping-stone to the university for such men as Samuel Taylor Coleridge, Charles Lamb, Leigh Hunt, Bishop Stillingfleet, and Samuel Richardson, who were students there.[3]

In choosing the S.P.G. as the trustee of his estate, Christopher Codrington had followed the well-established English practice of placing responsibility for an educational institution in the hands of an organized corporation—a pattern set in 1509 when John Colet, by his will, placed St. Paul's school under the management of the Mercers' Company. For the Empire, the project of founding Codrington College in the West Indies, against the background of a rapidly expanding society in Great Britain and the Colonies, had all the aspects of a pioneering adventure. Particularly valuable for today, therefore, are the careful records which, year by year, tell the story of the many large and small problems concerned with textbooks, schoolmasters, curriculum, selection of students, and the details of the budget of this new institution. In its temporary failures, as in its ultimate success, Codrington College has special significance as a first experiment in Empire education.

If the story of the college, like that of the plantation, during the eighteenth century is largely one of setbacks, it is likewise a commentary on the Society's positive goal that a casual reading of the Annual Reports to members rarely suggests that it was not a going concern throughout the whole period. Actually, an institution for higher learning was not opened until October 12, 1830. During the eighteenth century the grammar school, opened in 1745, performed the double function of serving as a testing ground for educational methods in the plantations and as a preparatory school for the college program which could be set up only as young men were schooled to meet its requirements.[4] By offering educational advantages to the young "men" of twelve, who might normally have gone to England, this grammar school was taking the first step toward the more ambitious program carried on in the next century.

Subject always to the fluctuations of the Codrington fund, this school achieved its greatest progress under Thomas Rotheram, 1745–1753; John Rotheram, 1753–1758; and James Butcher 1763–1775; and finally as reëstablished under Mark Nicholson who came to Barbados in 1797. From 1775 to 1786 no classes at all were held. But the corporation had an indestructible life, and, unlike a private enterprise, it could restore the buildings after hurricanes, supplement the Codrington funds after crop failures, and maintain its ideals in a hostile environment.

The delays in getting the school started were not always easy for the Barbadians to understand. They had been impressed with the early building efforts, but as hard times on the plantation delayed the actual opening of the school, they became skeptical. In 1724, Governor Henry Worsley expressed the sentiments of some of the planters when he wrote the Bishop of London that, although the college project was "highly commendable," the environment in Barbados made it "very difficult to educate Youth learnedly, or Virtuously."[5] Another citizen, more blunt than Governor Worsley, wrote with some derision of the plan for "your Chimerical College" and predicted an early failure of the entire project.[6]

Such views were not shared by all of the people, however. On March 4, 1729, the Society's attorney, Arthur Holt, urged the importance of a school for the white children of the island, and said of Barbadians in general:

> The People here seem more and more prejudiced against the notion which they have conceived of a College in this Island; but they generally wish for the Advantages of a well settled school to fit their Children for either of the Universities at Home, or qualifie them to go to any other Business. . . . Many say they wo'd then bring up their children to Letters, who will not Risque the Dangers of sending them to England for Education: and wo'd be willing to pay for their Accommodations on the Society's Estate, which wo'd not hinder the teaching of Paupers, nor the necessary Instruction of the Negroes. These are the general Sentiments of the people. . . .[7]

In 1742 a debt of £5,000 from the William Codrington estate was discharged and the prospects for opening the school looked brighter. By September, 1745, with its financial affairs somewhat cleared and the college buildings sufficiently completed, the school was opened. Thomas Rotheram, with a Master's degree from Queen's College, Oxford, and the Rev. Joseph Bewsher, A.B., had been appointed "To teach *gratis* twenty Children, the Sons of such Persons as shall be judged not to be in sufficient Circumstances to bring them up in learning the learned languages."[8]

Actually the educational facilities of Barbados unaided were insufficient to establish a collegiate institution, since such schools as existed were few, of low standards, and not college preparatory academies.[9] The Society's announcement recognized that the objects of the will were not thus being immediately fulfilled, but specified that the grammar school was opened so that "in time there may be Scholars ... properly qualified to receive the Instructions of the Professors hereafter to be chosen, who are to teach the Scholars Divinity, Physick, and Chirurgery...." As an English grammar school, then, the college was officially opened on September 9, 1745, and, from the first, it was referred to as "the College."[10]

This school was designed principally for boys under sixteen, and included two types of scholars. The "Gentlemen's Sons," whose status was the same as that of a boarder in the English schools, were supplied with room, board, books, and schooling upon the payment of a set sum.[11] The foundation scholars were the children of "such persons of good character, whose large families and narrow circumstances in life will not easily permit them to be at the whole expence of education themselves," and they were taught "gratis." The school opened with twelve foundation boys.[12] Before a month had passed, the number of charity students increased to seventeen. By August 13, 1746, the school also had ten paying boarders. For its commentary on conditions in Barbados, as well as its reflection of the methods of choosing foundation boys, the list of these seventeen students is here included. The average age was about ten. Four were orphans, six from neighboring parishes, and six were the sons of tenants or employees of the Society. There follows, on page 111, a list of these charity students by name, age, and parentage.[13]

1. Richard Harris	11	Son of Thomas Harris of the Parish of St. Lucy
2. Ralph Weeks	13	Son of Henry Weeks a Tenant to the Society's lower plantation
3. John Barlow	9	Orphan of the Parish of St. John
4. William Rogers	9	Son of Stephen Rogers of the parish of St. Philip
5. William Craggs	10	Orphan at the Parish of St. Andrew
6. Thomas Hall	10	Son of Samuel Hall of the Parish of St. Philip
7. Samuel Forte	9	Son of John Forte of the Parish of St. John
8. William Wilkey	12	Son of John Wilkey of the Parish of St. . . . .
9. William Souper	9	Son of Robert Souper of the Parish of St. Philip
10. William Southward	7½	Orphan of the Parish of St. James . . .
11. Samuel Eastmond	9	Orphan of the Parish of St. John . . .
12. Nicholas Gibbes	9	Son of Robert Gibbes, a Servant to the Society's lower Plantation
13. Walter Cason	7½	Son of John Cason, Clark of the Parish of St. John
14. James Howard	11 ⎫	Sons of James Howard ⎫ Tenants to
15. Anthony Howard	9 ⎭	⎪ the Society
16. Edward Marshal	10	Son of George Marshal ⎬
17. James Shepherd	10	Son of Nicholas Shepherd ⎭

With the beginning of class instruction, Rotheram as school-master and Bewsher as usher-catechist were confronted with the multiple tasks of organizing a curriculum, establishing academic standards, performing the administrative tasks, and building public good will. In some quarters it required all the tact of the masters, with the backing of Governor Henry Grenville, to counteract an attitude of suspended approval on the part of Barbadians.[14] During the first months of the school, the resentment over the full control of the school administration by the attorneys began to take form, and the schoolmasters wrote to England that their Barbadian trustees should "regard Punctilios less and essentials more."[15] Various plans were discussed during 1746, in which the faculty advocated complete separation of the school affairs from those of the plantation. The fact that eight of the students chosen by the attorneys without consulting the schoolmasters were dismissed from the school in 1747 as "Scholastically unsatisfactory" probably influenced the Society in its decision to place the estates largely in the hands of the schoolmasters, which was a policy effected in 1748.[16]

William Cattel had arrived in 1746 to act as surgeon and pharmacist, and also to instruct the scholars in these subjects as they became capable.[17] With the arrival in 1747 of William Bryant as "Professor of Philosophy and Mathematics," the staff was completed with four members.[18] Bewsher remained as catechist and Rotheram as master. Bryant and Cattel also held public lectures, similar to present-day extension courses, the masters at Codrington seemingly having this modern concept that educators should meet the needs of the community in addition to their class work. The lecture method itself was an innovation which had been introduced in the first decades of the eighteenth century. It is noteworthy that the Society should have established this method of instruction, since only the most progressive English schools had accepted the new technique, and Oxford and Cambridge, for the most part, used only the older tutorial method.[19]

The completion of the faculty and placement of control of the school administration in their hands signified a new period for the school. The first steps were directed toward obtaining a better student body. The islanders were advised by a notice, dated June 10, 1748, in the Barbados *Gazette* of the pending election of six foundation scholars to the Codrington school.[20] The candidates were required to be not more than twelve nor under seven years of age, proof of which must be presented. Further they must "be able to read the Bible distinctly."[20] Each boy was interviewed personally by the schoolmasters and admitted only on fulfillment of the qualifications. During the following years, all the vacancies were filled in this manner. In May 1748, an announcement made special provision for advanced instruction for students more than sixteen years of age, who were sufficiently schooled to attend the lectures of the professors, a first step toward the anticipated collegiate school.[21]

When a student was admitted to the foundation, the parent or guardian was required to subscribe to the explicit rules of the college.[22] There were two sets of rules, one for the foundation boys and one for the boarders. They were almost the same, and similar to the rules of such schools in England. Absence was allowed only with consent of the master or usher, and there was no excuse for missing Divine Service held every day. The boys were required to be pious in their speaking, and were prohibited from swearing, lying, or complaining. Equally stressed were the fundamentals of good manners, the students being warned to maintain a proper respect for their elders and to desist from speaking "rudely to strangers." Windows were a luxury made dearer by distance from the source of supply in England, and the boys were especially admonished not to break them. All infractions of these rules were handled by the faculty.[23]

The curriculum of the school, as with all schools of the period, laid particular stress on religious instruction. The first report of the staff gives an enlightening picture of the round of scholastic events. Thomas Rotheram wrote:

> We live in a very retired Manner, and much in a Collegiate Way. We begin the School at six in the Morning with that Particular Prayer appointed by the Society for Schoolmasters and their Scholars, together with the Lord's Prayer. We read the whole Morning service at eleven, and the whole Evening Service at five. On Sunday in the Morning we have Prayers and a Sermon, and Prayers in the Afternoon. . . .[24]

With the opening of the first term the nine boys who could read were put to work on grammar. Since the library had not yet been equipped, Rotheram wrote to London for texts. Among those listed were Corderius Colloquies, Justin, Phaedrus Fables, Ovid's Metamorphoses. These books had to come from England for there were no schoolbooks to be bought on the island.[25]

In 1747, with the arrival of the requested books, the class schedule had been formulated and Rotheram could report:

> We have reduced the Boys on the foundation into Two classes, seven in one and the remainder in another; the seven have gone through their Latin Grammar, and are reading Ovid's Metamorphoses and Justin: they are able with the Help of a Dictionary to render a Lesson in either of them very readily into English; and can make Latin very correctly as to Concord. and Grammar Rules; they are all very regular in their behaviour, and of tolerable Capacities. The others are in Turner's Exercise and Corderius; They have likewise gone through the Grammar; two of them, Hall and Southward, are very dull; but we must try what Industry and application will do sometime longer. I . . . shall be obliged to you if you will send the following, if the Society approve of them . . . Sallust, Virgil, Terence, Horace, [and the] Greek Grammar, common edition.[26]

In June 1748, plans were made to educate the scholars in the "sciences according to the established methods in the Universities in England." In this year, also, the surgeon and apothecary, Cattel, reported that some of the boys upon the foundation have made such progress in their learning, that they will soon become capable of receiving my Lectures," and for this purpose he asked that the Society "send over . . . the skeleton of an adult Person for the use of the College."[27]

The requests which went to England for books and supplies offer additional evidence of the activity of the pupils in the schools. On March 8, 1748, for instance, an order was sent for "a writing master's copy book, one of the most approved pieces in Book-keeping, and Bailey's English Dictionary."[28] Compasses, surveyors' chains, hydrostatic balances, reflecting telescopes, microscopes, barometers and thermometers, water pistons, glass tubes, and a magnifying glass were all requested by Bryant for his courses in mathematics and philosophy.[29]

The library, founded by the donations of Archbishop Thomas Tenison and other well-wishers, in 1783 had between eight and nine hundred books.[30] Both the school and the Society made an effort to maintain a library system. In 1753, books left to the college by Archbishop Tenison and a Rev. John Hill, were in England awaiting shipment. In a business-like manner, the Barbados committee in London recommended that these books be checked against the catalogue of the Codrington library and all duplicates sold so that the proceeds could be used to purchase other books.[31] Additions or bequests were made by the professors themselves when they left the college. The Rev. Thomas Falcon left his library valued at £300 to the college.

To continue with the progress of the school, in 1753 the Rev. John Rotheram, brother of Thomas, became master, and the Rev. Thomas Falcon, A.M., of Oxford, became usher. Already the inroads of disease and tropical conditions had made themselves felt in the Codrington faculty. In 1750, Bryant had died and Bewsher returned to England. In 1753, William Cattel and Thomas Rotheram also returned to England because of ill-health, leaving the school in charge of the two younger men. At first it was only a matter of continuing along the lines laid out by the founders, but hardly had John Rotheram and Falcon been installed when the Society felt the receipts of the plantation were not sufficient to support the continuance of a surgeon and a professor of mathematics and philosophy, and decreed a faculty of two members. Upon these two masters fell all the tasks of running the school and serving with others as attorneys for the plantations.

The problems of health, together with the remoteness of the college, added to the difficulties of the Society in obtaining replacements. Many young men, graduating from Oxford and Cambridge, were interested in teaching at Codrington, but the Society found that their parents were not willing to allow them to be exposed to the dangers of a distant and isolated tropical island. Despite the trouble in providing the college with a faculty, the number of pupils did not materially decrease.[33]

The high caliber of the men who did go out to teach at Codrington—in spite of disease, hurricanes, and financial difficulties—is revealed in their educational backgrounds. From Queen's College, Oxford, came Thomas Rotheram, master 1745–1753; John, his brother, usher 1751–1753 and master 1753–1758; Thomas Falcon, catechist 1753–1758 and master 1758–1762; John Hodgson, catechist 1759–1761, and Mark Nicholson, A.M., master 1797–1822. From St. John's, Cambridge, came William Bryant, professor of philosophy and mathematics from 1746 to his death in 1750, and James Butcher, master from 1763 to 1775.[34]

It is, perhaps, the best commentary on their ability to train men, that David Davies, one of the early students on the foundation, brought the school through more than a year almost single-handed. In 1761, on the death of the usher, Davies took over this job. In 1762, when Falcon died, and his successor, the Rev. Thomas Duke, resigned owing to bad health, Davies took charge of the school until 1763, when James Butcher arrived.[35]

The appointment of James Butcher, B.A., of St. John's, as headmaster, seemed to promise a partial fulfillment of the future prophesied by the Annual Reports throughout these dark years. Butcher was a native Barbadian, a fact which pleased the islanders. Under his management the school was to prosper for almost twelve years. The selection of Butcher had been preceded by the appointment in Barbados of a writing and arithmetic master. The office of usher had been vacant since 1761, and a replacement here also was anticipated. Meanwhile, Davies performed the duties with a "full allowance" from the Society of £70. Young Davies seems to have been a special favorite with Thomas Falcon who, on his death in 1762, left to Davies £200 and his horses, watch, and clothes.[36]

Under Butcher the rules of 1747 were revised.[37] The scholars continued to be divided into forms, and members of the highest form took turns serving as monitor, reporting all transgressions to the masters. As in Rotheram's day, school began every morning at six o'clock when the students were to be in class, their work having been prepared during the preceding evening. From six until nine they gave "due attendance to their lessons" and after breakfast they returned to their books until twelve, except on Wednesday, Friday, and Saints' days when they attended Divine Services. By two o'clock they were back at school and continued studying until five. Dinner was at seven in the evening and immediately afterwards the foundation scholars assembled for prayers, from whence they went to their "apartments and pass[ed] the night peaceably therein, without making any noise or disturbance."[38] Thus the schedule was strict, and little time was allowed for the boys to play at healthful exercise, or to get into trouble.

Affairs proceeded smoothly under Butcher for a time. The peaceful regime was marred by Davies' resignation in 1766. His action gives a glimpse of the absolute requirements for a teacher at Codrington, for in September, 1765, he wrote the Society of his inability to qualify for permanent office, because of the rule that the usher and master of the school must be in orders. His own examination of the tenets of the Anglican Church had convinced him that some of them were at the least "exceptionable," and that the Athanasian doctrine contradicted "both the obvious sense of Scripture, and the self-evident principles of reason."[39]

Beginning in 1770 the hard times in the islands and on the plantation inevitably affected the school. By August of 1773 Sir John Alleyne was writing the Society that the school had "sunk ... below its former reputation" and had never been comparable with the Rotheram school.[40] The expenses of running the college were becoming extremely high, and Butcher was in debt to the Society for the expenses of the boarders, which he had been unable to collect from impoverished parents. In taking steps to clear himself, he undertook the duties of St. John's parish in addition to his school responsibilities. By so doing he incurred the anger of Michael Mashart, the usher and catechist, who claimed prior right to the position. As a result Mashart withdrew from Codrington, and Butcher became involved in a long explanation of his action concerning St. John's. Finally, weighing the problems of personnel with those of finance, the Society determined to dispense with Codrington as a charity school for the time being, and in 1775, the foundation was closed, in spite of the protests of the attorneys, who wrote the Society that now "instead of shining in some Profession," the youth of Barbardos must needs "drudge on in the laborious walks of Life."[41]

Then in 1789, after thirteen years of quiet, Henry Husbands, who had been employed by the Society, without extra compensation, as catechist for the Negroes since 1786, started a school at the college for six white pupils chosen by the Society.[42] Whereas in the earlier school a full program including philosophy, divinity, and pharmacy had been offered, the curriculum for 1789 consisted of reading, writing, and arithmetic. The year 1791 saw an addition of six more boys to the foundation and the appointment of a writing master to assist Husbands, who was awarded an additional £50 in salary.[43] By 1795 eighteen boys were placed on the foundation, and the curriculum was broadened to include writing, English, arithmetic, and practical mathematics, and "If any boy discover marks of genius, at the request of the parents, he may be taught the learned languages." Husbands was followed as master in 1792 by the Rev. Clement B. Boucher. The Rev. William Thomas served from 1792 to 1796 and was followed by the Rev. Thomas Harrison Orderson, 1796–1797.[44]

The last decade of the century found the grammar school restored, funds increasing, and the foundation enrollment complete. The new regime was climaxed in 1797 when the Rev. Mark Nicholson, A.M., of Queen's College, Oxford, went out to Codrington with the title of President of the College and Superior Schoolmaster, at a salary of £200 per annum. At the same time Thomas Moody was appointed writing master.[45]

The Rev. William Harte became Nicholson's assistant in 1801.[46] In 1807, when J. Allinson succeeded William Harte as assistant master, boarders at the school were paying £60 to £70 a year with an extra fee of £5 for instruction in writing and £7 10s for special tutoring in mathematics. The daily routine of the school in July, 1807, is revealed in a contemporary account.

The boys on the foundation ... are either the sons of those parents who have large families, and who are but in middling circumstances, or the sons of decayed gentlemen. Their food consists of salt beef, salt pork, and such roots and vegetables as the estate produces, and whenever a hog or a sheep or an ox is killed upon the plantation, they always receive a part of it. They have chocolate, with ground provisions and salt fish for their breakfast and suppers. They lodge in one end of the College and the Boarders in the other. Some of them are taught the Latin and Greek languages: but the greater part have only Writing, Arithmetic, and English Grammar, and whatever may be thought most useful to them in their respective professions.[47]

Although the estates were producing modest profits, the trustees in London proceeded cautiously during this period in the expansion of the school, "their experience of the liabilities of a tropical climate have taught them not to rest the efficiency of the Institution upon the variable produce of the estates." Accordingly, they had determined not to proceed with large plans until the Codrington fund showed a funded capital of £20,000. When this sum was realized in 1813, another reorganization took place. It was decided that the benefits of the school should be restricted "to a higher class of Society," and it was ordered that every foundationer must "be the son of a Gentleman, a Clergyman, or of a Person, who with a large family or slender means may yet destine him for a liberal education." At the same time exhibitions of £100 for four years in England were established for such members of the school as showed themselves worthy.[48]

The founding of the bishopric of Barbados furnished the final catalyst required for realizing the old hope of a true West Indian college. Consecrated at Lambeth Palace on July 25, 1824, Bishop William Hart Coleridge landed, on January 29, 1825, in Barbados, the center of a diocese which included the Leeward Islands and British Guiana.[49] He found the school under the direction of the Rev. Henry Parkinson, who had succeeded to the principalship after Nicholson (1797–1821) and the Rev. Samuel Hinds (1821–

1824). Parkinson was to be followed by the first principal of Codrington as a true college, the Rev. John Hothersall Pinder (1829–1835). Pinder, a native of the island, had served as catechist to the Negroes.[50]

Meanwhile Bishop Coleridge was busily extending the educational advantages of the island in general,[51] but with particular care in the affairs of the college. A report of 1825 may be quoted here at some length for its picture of the projects afoot and of the mood of the island:

There is, my Lord, a strong feeling in the Island that some decided improvements and on a large scale are intended at the College and I have not contradicted the report; it would be received with great delight, as tending to raise the Island of Barbados in the West Indian scale, and conferring important benefits on the Island itself, and I consider that I may safely say that there would be no objection on their part to admit of an extension of these benefits to the whole of the Leeward Islands.

If your Lordship should ask in what way the college might be made more effectual than it now is, I would venture to reply—by placing at its head a man of talent and activity and he would find the situation full of more comforts than he expects, and worthy of all his exertions and under him two or three tutors, and the proposed buildings would be capable of holding fifty students to be sent to this College for the completion of their education from the private schools in this and the other Islands.[52]

A visitor to Barbados, Henry Nelson Coleridge, the Bishop's nephew, reviewed the state of education at the college in his *Six Months in the West Indies in 1825*. He was concerned to find that "so magnificent a charity and such large actual funds ... originally intended as a university for youths and not a mere school for boys," was furnishing only "the support and instruction of fourteen or fifteen boys, who might be educated much better elsewhere in the island." He was aware that the deficiencies he described had, for some time "been the subject of inquiry and deliberation to the Society," but he concluded his friendly indictment with the charge that, for all practical purposes the members' "Disinterestedness is perfect, their intentions excellent."[53] The Bishop had himself been concerned with the state of education at the school. In a private letter to the Secretary of the Society, he discussed the necessary reforms. He noted that the papers submitted in an examination in Latin were "distressingly bad."[54]

The rapid progress made as a result of such proddings, with the presence of the Bishop, and with growing profits from the estate, is reflected in the subsequent correspondence. Plans were suggested and projects completed in terms of the Bishop's regular visits. On September 1, 1829, the first meeting of the College Council was called with Bishop Coleridge in attendance. Edward Parris Smith, the tutor, reported that he had already started upon a program of lectures to such young men as had expressed a wish to attend, using the Greek Testament and Hey's lectures on the Articles, for the Senior class; Herodotus and the *Antigone* of Sophocles for the second class, and the Odes of Horace and the Gospel of St. Matthew for the junior class.[55] In July, 1830, twenty-six students were in attendance and plans were proceeding for the formal opening of the college.[56]

Finally, on September 9, 1830, with Bishop Coleridge presiding, the college was formally opened. An oration in honor of the founder, delivered by a student whose composition had been judged best, and proper exercises including religious services, completed the day. In accordance with the will of the founder, the medical and surgical sciences formed a part of the curriculum, along with mathematics and natural philosophy.[57] A glimpse of the students at work is afforded by careful accounts to the Society of the college routine.[58] In addition to the regular lectures, the senior students were frequently examined on sections of the Gospel, which they were expected to prepare for the lecture. Paley's *Horae Paulinae* was a subject of daily examination until it was finished, and other branches of theology added to thorough instruction in ecclesiastical history.[59]

On July 7, 1834, four years after the opening of the college, Pinder could report to the Society that four classical schoolmasters from among the Codrington students had already been placed. S. A. Farr was serving as second master in the Society's grammar school and F. K. Braithwaite was acting as a headmaster in Antigua. Of Farr's predecessors at the Codrington grammar school R. J. Rock was ordained for Grenada, and Duncan Gittens had proceeded to England "to enter at the University of Oxford." Meanwhile, Samuel P. Musson and William A. Beckles were awaiting appointments as readers to rectors in Berbice and Nevis, respectively. Two of the ten exhibitioners were preparing for the next ordination, and "Three of the five commoners are candidates for orders." Two of the students planned during the next year to remove to Oxford or Cambridge, and a third planned to pursue "eventually his medical studies in England," and another was preparing for the law.[60] Thus it may be seen that the hurricane of 1831, which seriously damaged the college buildings, seems in no way to have interfered with progress in the schoolroom.[61]

Although the compass of this book is limited largely to the period before 1834, a quick glance ahead will enable the reader to judge the success of the college as it was finally established. Altogether, 390 students were trained at Codrington between 1830 and 1900, of whom 10 per cent were Negroes and 94 received degrees of M.A. or B.A. Three-fifths of the clergymen in the West Indies had received some education at the college, and colored missionaries had been sent to other islands in the Indies and to West Africa. Indeed, by the middle of the nineteeth century the Society could report that the supply of missionaries for the Americas and the West Indies was no longer coming principally from the Mother Country, since the establishment of colleges of classical and theological education in all the provinces of British North America, had, to a great degree, superseded the necessity of sending clergymen from England. Codrington College was thus the parent of those schools in Windsor, Fredericton, Cobourg, and Lennoxville which, according to C. F. Pascoe, were, in 1900, "yearly supplying candidates for the ministry . . . better trained for the work . . . in their own country by being hardened to its climate, and inured to the privations and hardships which belong to new settlements.[62]

Thus the first 120 years of Codrington school were, in reality, charting a course for today's educational institutions in the British colonies. Caldecott suggests that Codrington's vision of a college stimulated Berkeley in his later efforts, and points to the fact that Coleridge and Pinder, Codrington founders, transferred their efforts to England, where Coleridge served as the first warden of the first English missionary college, St. Augustine's in Canterbury; and Pinder became the first principal of Wells, "the most successful of all the Theological colleges."[63]

Though funds were often greatly depleted, though illness and death took their toll of teachers and pupils, and college buildings seemed no sooner built than they were destroyed, the school provided for in the will of Christopher Codrington, sometime soldier, poet, book collector, and bachelor, became a notable institution in tropical America. Codrington College was a pioneer in testing and adapting known English curricula and methods of instruction to the Negroes and the whites in the colonial world, first in a slave economy and then among free men. In spite of typhoon, lukewarm friends, and "the blasts" of the seasons, the S.P.G. stayed with its task until, aided by the new humanitarianism in Britain, better days came with the dawn of the nineteenth century.

NOTES

NOTES TO THE INTRODUCTION

[1] Quotations from the Annual Sermon of Bishop William Fleetwood, February 16, 1711, in Frank J. Klingberg, *Anglican Humanitarianism in Colonial New York* (Philadelphia, 1940), pp. 210–211; complete sermon, pp. 196–212. See also "Leading Ideas in the Annual S.P.G. Sermons," *ibid.*, pp. 11–48.

[2] For a more detailed discussion of the influence of the Society, see Klingberg, *Contributions of the S. P. G. to the American Way of Life* (Philadelphia, 1943).

[3] Otis P. Starkey, *The Economic Geography of Barbados* (New York, 1939), "A Chronological Chart Showing the Principle Variable Factors Influencing the Development of Barbados, 1627–1735," pp. 8–9, gives the sugar exports and sugar prices in London. An excellent work.

NOTES TO CHAPTER I

OF THE NOBLE AND GENEROUS BENEFACTION OF

GENERAL CHRISTOPHER CODRINGTON

[1] Dudley Woodbridge and Gilbert Ramsay to S.P.G. Secretary, Barbados, June 20, 1711, S.P.G. Manuscripts (Library of Congress Transcripts), Volume A, No. 6, pp. 333–338. Hereafter cited as S.P.G. MSS (L.C. Trans.).

[2] For the full text of the will, see Vincent T. Harlow, *Christopher Codrington, 1668–1710* (Oxford, 1928), pp. 217–220.

[3] Montagu Burrows, *Worthies of All Souls; Four Centuries of English History, Illustrated from the College Archives* (London, 1874), p. 328.

[4] *Ibid.*, p. 329.

[5] *Caribbeana. Containing Letters and Dissertations, Together with Poetical Essays, on various Subjects and Occasions; Chiefly wrote by several Hands in the West Indies*, 2 vols. (London, 1741). The entry for Wednesday, October 8, 1735, Vol. II, pp. 96–99, resurrects a fragment of General Codrington's writings "indisputably genuine," to enforce arguments against usurpation by the then governor of unreasonable power. Codrington's paper on the power of a colonial governor emphasizes the constitutional rights of all Englishmen and comments, "The Constitution . . . is very much in some Men's Mouths, but little in their Hearts, and less in their Understandings, since they sacrifice it so often to Spite, Passion, Pride, Caprice, and private Interest. . . ."

[6] Harlow, *op. cit., passim.*

[7] Sir John Robert Seeley, *The Expansion of England* (London, 1898), pp. 154–155.

[8] For further studies of the life and activities of Thomas Bray, see Samuel Clyde McCulloch, "The Foundation and Early Work of the Society for the Propagation of the Gospel in Foreign Parts," *The Huntington Library Quarterly*, VIII (1945), pp. 241–258; *idem*, "Dr. Thomas Bray's Final Years at Aldgate," *The Historical Magazine of the Protestant Episcopal Church*, XIV (1945), pp. 322–336; *idem*, "Dr. Thomas Bray's trip to Maryland: A Study in Militant Anglican Humanitarianism," *William and Mary Quarterly*, 3d ser., II (1945), pp. 15–32; and *idem*, "The Importance of Dr. Thomas Bray's *Bibliotheca Parochialis*," *The Historical Magazine of the Protestant Episcopal Church*, XV (1946), pp. 50–59.

[9] S.P.G. Journal (Library of Congress Photostat), Vol. 1, pp. 1–2. Hereafter cited as S.P.G. Journal (L.C. Photo), Vol. 1, pp. 1–2.

[10] *Ibid.*, pp. 3–4.

[11] *Twelve Anniversary Sermons Preached before the Society for the Propagation of the Gospel in Foreign Parts* (London, 1845), p. 17. For a complete printing of the charter, see *A Collection of Papers Printed by Order of the Society for the Propagation of the Gospel in Foreign Parts* (London, 1714). Hereafter cited as *A Collection of S.P.G. Papers.*

[12] For a detailed study of the program for Negroes in two of the American colonies, see Frank J. Klingberg, *Anglican Humanitarianism in Colonial New York* (Philadelphia, 1940), and *idem, An Appraisal of the Negro in Colonial South Carolina* (Washington, D.C., 1941).

[13] J. C. Wippell, "Codrington College," in James Ebenezer Reece and Charles Guilding Clark-Hunt, eds., *Barbados Diocesan History* (London, 1928), p. 65.

[14] Klingberg, *Anglican Humanitarianism,* p. 48.

[15] S.P.G. Journal (L.C. Photo), Vol. 1, p. 7. The sum was £56.1.6 for the printing.

[16] *Ibid.*, p. 10.

[17] *An Account of the Society for Propagating the Gospel in Foreign Parts* (London, 1706), p. 4.

[18] For this figure and the following statistics, see the Table of Income and Expenditures, 1701–1893, given in *Classified Digest of the Records of the Society for the Propagation of the Gospel in Foreign Parts* (London, 1893), pp. 830–832.

[19] C. F. Pascoe, *Two Hundred Years of the S.P.G.,* 2 vols. (London, 1901), II, pp. 830–831.

[20] For a treatment of this subject, see Alfred W. Newcombe, "The Appointment and Instruction of S.P.G. Missionaries," *Church History,* V (December, 1936), pp. 340–358.

[21] *A Collection of S.P.G. Papers,* p. 9.

[22] S.P.G. Journal (L.C. Photo), Vol. 1, p. 158.

[23] Newcombe, *loc. cit.,* p. 346.

[24] *Ibid.*

[25] "An Abstract of the most Remarkable Proceedings and Occurrences of the Society for the Propagation of the Gospel in Foreign Parts from February 15, 1711/12 to February 20, 1712/13," printed with John Moore, *Sermon Preached before the Society for the Propagation of the Gospel in Foreign Parts at their Anniversary Meeting in the Parish Church of St. Mary-le-Bow, on Friday the 20th of February 1712/13* (London, 1713), pp. 32–33. Hereafter cited as Abstract of S.P.G. Proceedings, printed with Annual *Sermon,* 1713. The date hereafter used for any Sermon will be the year of delivery, not the year of publication.

[26] *Ibid.*

[27] For a copy of this record, see Pascoe, *op. cit.,* II, pp. 836–840.

[28] Thomas Secker, *A Sermon Preached before the Incorporated Society for the Propagation of the Gospel in Foreign Parts: at their Anniversary Meeting in the Parish Church of St. Mary-le-Bow, on Friday, February 20, 1740* (London, 1741), pp. 13–14. Hereafter cited as Secker, Annual *Sermon, 1740.*

[29] S.P.G. meeting, London, October 20, 1710, S.P.G. Journal (L.C. Photo), Vol. 1, pp. 504–521; further meetings, January 5, 1711 and February 8, 1711, *ibid.,* pp. 548–573; Dudley Woodbridge and Gilbert Ramsay to S.P.G. Secretary, Barbados, July 17, 1711, S.P.G. MSS (L.C. Trans.), A 6, pp. 341–344.

[30] Abstract of S.P.G. Proceedings, printed with Annual *Sermon*, 1712, pp. 36–38; Dudley Woodbridge to S.P.G. Secretary, Barbados, March 15, 1712, Misc. Unbound Docs. (L.C. film), IX, pt. 1, pp. 269–284; notes on the dispute between William Codrington and the Society, London [1741], S.P.G. MSS (L.C. Trans.), B 8, pp. 150–164.

[31] Abstract of S.P.G. Proceedings, printed with Annual *Sermon*, 1712, pp. 36–38.

[32] The estimated expense of constructing the college was £12,000, according to the estimate of Bishop Robert Drummond in 1760. Bishop of St. Asaph to Archbishop of Canterbury, London, March 15, 1760, Lambeth Palace MSS (L.C. Trans.), 1123, pt. 2, No. 171.

[33] Dudley Woodbridge to S.P.G. Secretary, Barbados, March 15, 1715, Misc. Un. Docs. (L.C. film), IX, pt. 1, pp. 269–284.

[34] Minutes of the S.P.G. meeting, London, October 19, 1711, S.P.G. Journal (L.C. Photo), Vol. 2, pp. 96–109. William Codrington to his agents, Barbados, October 30, 1711, Misc. Un. Docs. (L.C. film), IX, pt. 2, pp. 205–206. Dudley Woodbridge to S.P.G. Secretary, Barbados, March 15, 1712, Misc. Un. Docs. (L.C. film), IX, pt. 1, pp. 269–284. Notes on the dispute with William Codrington, London [1741], S.P.G. MSS (L.C. Trans.), B 8, pp. 150–164. Philip Bearcroft to Abel Alleyne, London, January 7, 1743, S.P.G. MSS (L.C. Trans.), B 8, pp. 235–237.

[35] *Ibid.;* Observation on the agreement with William Codrington, London, August 30, 1712, Misc. Un. Docs. (L.C. film), XIII, pp. 168–172.

[36] Abstract of S.P.G. Proceedings, printed with Annual *Sermon*, 1713, pp. 68–69.

[37] Burrows, *op. cit.*, p. 341.

NOTES TO CHAPTER II

OF THE BUILDINGS IN PROGRESS WITH WHICH
TO HOUSE THE COLLEGE

[1] Abstract of S.P.G. Proceedings, printed with Annual *Sermon*, 1714, p. 52.

[2] *Ibid.*

[3] *Ibid.*, pp. 36–37.

[4] Sir Robert H. Schomburgk, *The History of Barbados; Comprising a Geographical and Statistical Description of the Islands; A Sketch of the Historical Events since the Settlement; And an Account of its Geology and Natural Products* (London, 1848), p. 232.

[5] Abstract of S.P.G. Proceedings, printed with Annual *Sermon*, 1712, pp. 67–70. Colonel Codrington had also furnished "... as much *New England* Timber as would repair all the buildings" for seven years to come; Antigua timber to supply the mills and carts, and 500 guineas to buy books.

[6] *Ibid.*, 1715, p. 56.

[7] *Ibid.*, 1716, p. 34.

[8] *Ibid.*, pp. 33–34.

[9] *Ibid.*, 1715, pp. 53–54.

[10] *Ibid.*, pp. 54–55.

[11] *Ibid.*, 1717, p. 38.

¹² *Ibid.*, 1715, p. 59. "Orders are issued to send forthwith 100,000 more than the 600,000 well-burnt *Bricks already gone,* with the 20 Chaldron of *Coals* brought in the Pool, and 2 Tons of *Iron Bars* sotted."

¹³ *Ibid.*, 1717, p. 38. The Society had to "procure an Order from the Admiralty Board to the present Commander of the *Stationary* Man of War for that Island, to Assist the Society's Agents, when it can be done without Prejudice to his Majesty's Service, in fetching of Timber from the Adjacent Islands within the Jurisdiction of the Government of *Barbadoes.*"

¹⁴ *Ibid.*, 1718, p. 39. Another report added, "The Buildings on the Plantations are now compleat, and in very good repair, and there is now no Occasion for new ones."

¹⁵ *Ibid.*, 1715, p. 54.

¹⁶ *Ibid.*, 1720, p. 54. "The stones ... are ... sawed out of a Hill just before the Front, and are capable of being cut into what Moulding they please; and by being exposed to the Weather they grow extremely hard."

¹⁷ John Smalridge to S.P.G. Secretary, Barbados, June 4, 1725, Misc. Un. Docs. (L.C. film), IX, pt. 1, p. 76. Smalridge added, "I shall write by him to the Society from whom they may learn a particular account of what related to the work of the College—so they will the better know how to proceed." College accounts for 1725, Barbados, July 20, 1725, Misc. Un. Docs. (L.C. film), IX, pt. 1, pp. 57–61.

¹⁸ Dudley Woodbridge to S.P.G. Secretary, Barbados, April 9, 1715, Misc. Un. Docs. (L.C. film), I 4, p. 73.

¹⁹ College accounts for 1725, Barbados, July 20, 1725, Misc. Un. Docs. (L.C. film), IX, pt. 1, p. 61.

²⁰ *Ibid.* John Smalridge to S.P.G. Secretary, Barbados, July 25, 1728, Misc. Un. Docs. (L.C. film), XII, pp. 241–242.

²¹ Charles Cunningham to S.P.G. Secretary, Barbados, September 20, 1717, Fulham Palace MSS, (L.C. Trans.), "Barbadoes," No. 104.

²² Abstract of S.P.G. Proceedings, printed with Annual *Sermon,* 1720, pp. 54–55.

²³ *Ibid.*, 1722, pp. 52–53.

²⁴ Instructions for finishing the chapel, London, March 2, 1722, Misc. Un. Docs. (L.C. film), XIII, pp. 136–137.

²⁵ Meeting of the S.P.G., London, May 19, 1721, S.P.G. Journal (L.C. film), Vol. 4, pp. 162–163.

²⁶ Abstract of S.P.G. Proceedings, printed with Annual *Sermon,* 1722, p. 45.

²⁷ *Ibid.*, 1723, pp. 52–53.

²⁸ *Ibid.*, 1721, pp. 45–46.

²⁹ John Smalridge to S.P.G. Secretary, Barbados, April 13, 1724, Misc. Un. Docs. (L.C. film), IX, pt. 1, p. 22.

³⁰ *Ibid.*, Barbados, July 25, 1724, Misc. Un. Docs. (L.C. film), IX, pt. 1, p. 16.

³¹ Abstract of S.P.G. Proceedings, printed with Annual *Sermon,* 1722, p. 52.

³² *Ibid.*, 1726, pp. 41–42. A Memorandum, dated September 17, 1725, Misc. Un. Docs. (L.C. film), West Indies, XIII, pp. 158–159, notes that the college was "covered" but further supplies were required for the chapel including:

1800 ft of Carolina Cedar Plank for the fronts and lineings of the ... Seats 600 ft of which to be Inch and half and 1200 ft ¾ of an Inch thick.
200 ft of Two Inch ditto for Mouldings
250 yellow deals slit for Coveing

The outer door of the Chappel and Hall may be made of Cedar w'ch may be had in the Island; it being difficult to be got of a sufficient length from Carolina.

Steps also were needed for the vestibule, Chapel and Hall and pavement for the vestibule and passages. If deals were to be furnished for the lodgings, it was observed, it would be much cheaper to send them from England than to buy them in Barbados.

[33] Plantation Accounts for 1725, Misc. Un. Docs. (L.C. film), XII, pp. 99–131.

[34] John Smalridge to S.P.G. Secretary, Barbados, July 20, 1725, Misc. Un. Docs. (L.C. film), IX, pt. 1, pp. 65–66.

[35] Arthur Holt to Bishop of London, Barbados, November 17, 1730, Fulham Palace MSS (L.C. film), No. 84.

[36] Minutes of Attorneys, Barbados, April 6, 1731, Fulham Palace MSS (L.C. Trans.), "Barbadoes," No. 81.

[37] Plantation Accounts for 1720, Misc. Un. Docs. (L.C. film), XII, pp. 67–81.

January 1, 1719	Paid for pipe of Wine	18/–/–
	7 pewter Dishes	2/4/11
	Pipe of Wine	14/1/3
	Small case of Pickles	/14/4
August 19, 1720	A pipe of Wine	18/–/–
Sept. 4, 1720	12 silverspoons and marking them	13/2/6
	For Sundays when the President mett with the Comis. Attorneys	9/15/3½

[38] *Ibid.*, p. 73.

[39] Meeting of Attorneys, Barbados, March 22, 1745, Misc. Un. Docs. (L.C. film), IX, pt. 2, pp. 181–182.

[40] *Ibid.*, p. 182.

[41] Thomas Rotheram to S.P.G. Secretary, Barbados, December 7, 1746, Misc. Un. Docs. (L.C. film), IX, pt. 2, pp. 232–236.

[42] John Payne to S.P.G. Secretary, Barbados, December 14, 1746, Misc. Un. Docs. (L.C. film), IX, pt. 2, p. 89.

[43] *Ibid.*, Barbados, December 5, 1746, Misc. Un. Docs. (L.C. film), IX, pt. 2, p. 91.

[44] Joseph Bewsher to S.P.G. Secretary, August 4, 1747, Misc. Un. Docs. (L.C. film), VIII, pp. 249–252; also in IX, pt. 1, pp. 106–109.

[45] William Bryant to S.P.G. Secretary, Barbados, July 6, 1747, Misc. Un. Docs. (L.C. film), VIII, pp. 47–50.

[46] The reports for July 4 and 5, 1751, August 15, 1751, July 2, 1753 are typical of those which were concerned entirely with plantation affairs and made no mention of the college. For these reports, see Misc. Un. Docs. (L.C. film), IX, pt. 1, pp. 166–170, 245–248, 318, 319.

[47] Bishop of St. Asaph to Archbishop of Canterbury, March 15, 1760, Lambeth Palace MSS (L.C. Trans.), 1123, pt. 2, No. 171. *Ibid.*, February 29, 1760, No. 168.

[48] Abstract of S.P.G. Proceedings, printed with Annual *Sermon*, 1781, p. 45.

[49] *Ibid.*, 1795, pp. 56–57.

[50] Pascoe, *op. cit.*, I, 200.

[51] Bishop of Barbados to Bishop of London, April 27, 1825, Fulham Palace MSS (L.C. Trans.), "Barbadoes," No. 157.

[52] John Pinder to S.P.G. Secretary, Barbados, July 14, 1830, Misc. Un. Docs. (L.C. film), VIII, pp. 260–261.

[53] Pascoe, *op. cit.*, II, p. 782.

[54] *Ibid.*, I, p. 394.

[55] Reece and Clark-Hunt, *op. cit.*, p. 67.

NOTES TO CHAPTER III

OF THE PLANTATIONS INTIRE

[1] Dudley Woodbridge and Gilbert Ramsay to S.P.G. Secretary, Barbados, January 10, 1713, Misc. Un. Docs. (L.C. film), West Indies, IX, pt. 1, pp. 290–302.

[2] The figures on the sizes of the estates vary. In a memorandum of May 16, 1733 [Fulham Palace MSS (L.C. Trans.), "Barbadoes," No. 71] a detailed breakdown of the acreages on the estates is given. The upper estate consisted of 270 acres, of which 140–160 were planted in first- and second-crop canes and the remainder chiefly in guinea corn. On the lower estate, consisting of 480 acres, only 60 acres were on a level to operate a cart, 25 of which were usually planted. More than 200 acres are described as "all waste in chalkie hills and paths."

[3] Thomas Rotheram to Dr. Bearcroft, Barbados, December 7, 1746, Misc. Un. Docs. (L.C. film), West Indies, IX, pt. 2, p. 236, and William Bryant to Dr. Bearcroft, Barbados, September 23, 1747, *ibid.*, VIII, pp. 40–41.

[4] John Smalridge to David Humphreys, Barbados, October 12, 1724, Misc. Un. Docs. (L.C. film), West Indies, IX, pt. 1, pp. 4–5.

[5] Selections from this correspondence are reproduced in John A. Schutz and Maud O'Neil, "Arthur Holt, Anglican Clergyman, Reports on Barbados, 1725–1733," *The Journal of Negro History*, XXXI (October, 1946), pp. 444–469.

[6] Arthur Holt to Bishop of London, Barbados, April 9, 1731, Fulham Palace MSS (L.C. Trans.), "Barbadoes," No. 88.

[7] Joseph Bewsher to S.P.G. Secretary, September 28, 1747, Misc. Un. Docs. (L.C. film), West Indies, VIII, pp. 32–33.

[8] Draft of a Letter from the Society to its Attorneys in Barbados [March 15], 1760, Lambeth Palace MSS (L.C. Trans.), 1123, pt. 2, No. 172.

[9] John Smalridge to George Smalridge, Barbados, March 23, 1711, S.P.G. MSS (L.C. Trans.), A 6, pp. 214–215.

[10] John Smalridge to David Humphreys, Barbados, October 12, 1724, Misc. Un. Docs. (L.C. film), West Indies, IX, pt. 1, p. 5.

[11] S.P.G. Journal (L.C. Photo), XIV, p. 181.

[12] Attorneys to S.P.G. Secretary, Barbados, July 16, 1761, Misc. Un. Docs. (L.C. film), West Indies, IX, pt. 1, p. 350.

[13] In 1748 Thomas Rotheram pointed out that the sum paid out in annual rental for Negroes would cover the purchase price of the same number of slaves in a few years. See Thomas Rotheram to S.P.G. Secretary, Barbados, June 20, 1748, *ibid.*, pp. 182–185.

[14] Plantation accounts for 1812, Misc. Un. Docs. (L.C. film), X, p. 58.

[15] Attorneys to S.P.G. Secretary, Barbados, July 10, 1760, Misc. Un. Docs. (L.C. film), IX, pt. 2, p. 148.

[16] S.P.G. Journal (L.C. Photo), Vol. 14, pt. 3, p. 273.

[17] Attorney to S.P.G. Secretary, Barbados, July 11, 1761, Misc. Un. Docs. (L.C. film), IX, pt. 1, p. 350.

[18] *Ibid.*

[19] Codrington Attorneys to S.P.G. Secretary, Barbados, May 28, 1762, S.P.G. MSS (L.C. Trans.), B 6, pt. 1, p. 248.

[20] Society's Attorneys to S.P.G. Secretary, Barbados, July 11, 1761, Misc. Un. Docs. (L.C. film), IX, pt. 1, pp. 347–353.

²¹ S.P.G. Journal (L.C. Photo), Vol. 2, p. 64. John Smalridge's letter was discussed at the meeting of the Society on June 22, 1711.

²² Abstract of S.P.G. Proceedings, printed with Annual *Sermon*, 1714, p. 52; *ibid.*, 1715, p. 52.

²³ John Smalridge to S.P.G. Secretary, Barbados, October 12, 1724, Misc. Un. Docs. (L.C. film), IX, pt. 1. pp. 4–5. Smalridge added: "These two last crops have been tolerable but the charges run high which is not to be avoided where a plantation is under stockd as this is and so very laborious."

²⁴ *Ibid.*, p. 5.

²⁵ *Ibid.*, April 13, 1724, p. 22.

²⁶ *Ibid.*, p. 66. On December 31, 1724, the Society's labor force included 224 Negroes and 108 cattle. See Plantation accounts for 1725, Misc. Un. Docs. (L.C. film), XII, p. 130.

²⁷ Arthur Holt to S.P.G. Secretary, Barbados, April 9, 1733, Fulham Palace MSS (L.C. Trans.), "Barbadoes," No. 69. The 25 acres of canes on the lower estate "must be carried up to the work by asses but chiefly by negroes which is so laborious it does not answer but makes the negroes run away."

²⁸ John Smalridge to S.P.G. Secretary, Barbados, June 27, 1728, Misc. Un. Docs. (L.C. film), XIII, p. 125.

²⁹ Plantation accounts for 1719, Misc. Un. Docs. (L.C. film), XII, p. 90

³⁰ John Smalridge to S.P.G. Secretary, Barbados, July 25, 1728, Misc. Un. Docs. (L.C. film), XII, pp. 241–242.

³¹ Arthur Holt to Bishop of London, Barbados, August 16, 1732, Fulham Palace MSS (L.C. Trans.), "Barbadoes," No. 68.

³² *Ibid.*

³³ William Johnson to Bishop of London, Barbados, May 29, 1730, Fulham Palace MSS (L.C. Trans.), "Barbadoes," No. 82. "... the inhabitants ... oppose paying ... the King's tax.... The chief promoters ... are the representatives and vestries ... of the parishes."

³⁴ Arthur Holt to Bishop of London, Barbados, November 17, 1730, Fulham Palace MSS (L.C. Trans.), "Barbadoes," No. 84.

³⁵ Meeting of Attorneys, Barbados, April 6, 1731, Fulham Palace MSS (L.C. Trans.), "Barbadoes," No. 81.

³⁶ Arthur Holt to Bishop of London, Barbados, October 4, 1731, Fulham Palace MSS (L.C. Trans.), "Barbadoes," No. 61. Enemies of Worsley beset the Rev. Mr. Johnson "with swords, pistols, and beat of drums.... [Holt and his wife] was awakened with terrible noise of the broken sash windows, rock stones and clubs flying about the house...."

³⁷ *Ibid.*, December 2, 1730, No. 78.

³⁸ *Ibid.*, July 3, 1731, No. 63.

³⁹ *Ibid.*, July 3, 1731, No. 63.

⁴⁰ *Ibid.* [November 17, 1730], No. 84.

⁴¹ *Ibid.*, May 2, 1733, No. 70.

⁴² Meeting of Attorneys, Barbados, March 21 and 22, 1745, Misc. Un. Docs. (L.C. film), IX, pt. 2, p. 180.

⁴³ *Ibid.*, May 26, 1748, Misc. Un. Docs. (L.C. film), VIII, p. 27; *ibid.*, March 4, 1751, IX, pt. 1, p. 241.

⁴⁴ *Ibid.*, September 6 and 7, 1748, VIII, pp. 24–25.

⁴⁵ William Bryant to S.P.G. Secretary, Barbados, March 23, 1749, Misc. Un. Docs. (L.C. film), IX, pt. 2, p. 184.

⁴⁶ Meeting of Codrington Attorneys, September 1 and 7, 1748, Misc. Un. Docs. (L.C. film), VIII, p. 16.

[47] Thomas Barnard and Thomas Rotheram to S.P.G. Secretary, Barbados, August 24, 1750, Misc. Un. Docs. (L.C. film), IX, pt. 1, p. 252.

[48] John Rotheram to S.P.G. Secretary, Barbados, July 2, 1753, Misc. Un. Docs. (L.C. film), IX, pt. 1, pp. 317–318.

[49] *Ibid.*, January 29, 1753, IX, pt. 1, p. 321.

[50] John Rotheram to Philip Bearcroft, Barbados, July 2, 1753, Misc. Un. Docs. (L.C. film), IX, pt. 1, p. 318.

[51] Report on condition of the estates, January 26, 1760, Lambeth Palace MSS (L.C. Trans.), 1123, pt. 2, No. 162. Bishop of St. Asaph to Archbishop of Canterbury, London, March 15, 1760, Lambeth Palace MSS (L.C. Trans.), 1123, pt. 2, No. 171.

[52] Meeting of the Society, London, March 21, 1760, S.P.G. Journal (L.C. film), XIV, p. 264; another meeting, April 18, 1760, *ibid.*, pp. 266–274.

[53] *Ibid.*, pp. 266–274.

[54] Bishop of St. Asaph to Archbishop of Canterbury, March 15, 1760, Lambeth Palace MSS (L.C. Trans.), 1123, pt. 2, No. 171.

[55] Attorneys to S.P.G. Secretary, Barbados, July 11, 1761, Misc. Un. Docs. (L.C. film), IX, pt. 1, p. 349.

[56] *Ibid.*

[57] *Ibid.*, July 10, 1760, IX, pt. 2, pp. 144–149; recommendations for leasing the estates, London, March 11, 1760, Lambeth Palace MSS (L.C. Trans.), 1123, pt. 2, No. 170.

[58] S.P.G. meeting, London, December 19, 1766, S.P.G. Journal, Vol. 17, pp. 184–212; another meeting, November 20, 1767, *ibid.*, pp. 384–398.

[59] Attorneys to S.P.G. Secretary, Barbados, August 13, 1767, Misc. Un. Docs. (L.C. film), XIII, p. 61.

[60] Sir John Alleyne to S.P.G. Secretary, Barbados, June 2, 1774, S.P.G. MSS (L.C. Trans.), B 6, pt. 1, pp. 382–385.

[61] For full details of the various plans suggested in Barbados and in London for resolving these difficulties, see S.P.G. MSS (L.C. Trans.), B 6, pt. 1, pp. 345–351, 354, 378, 382–388, 414–422; T. Herbert Bindley, *Annals of Codrington College Barbados, 1710–1910* (London, 1910), p. 25.

[62] *Gentleman's Magazine*, LI (January, 1781), pp. 43–44.

[63] Abstract of S.P.G. Proceedings, printed with Annual *Sermon*, 1781, pp. 45–46.

[64] Minutes of Codrington Attorneys, October 6 and 7, 1777, Misc. Un. Docs. (L.C. film), XIII, p. 22.

[65] Thomas Rotheram to S.P.G. Secretary, Barbados, October 7, 1745, Misc. Un. Docs. (L.C. film), IX, pt. 1, p. 362.

[66] Pascoe, *op. cit.*, p. 198.

[67] *Ibid.;* notes on Braithwaite negotiation, London, 1782–1783, Misc. Un. Docs. (L.C. film), American Colonies, Vouchers, 1785, pp. 290–304.

[68] Clearances of Society's estates, Misc. Un. Docs. (L.C. film), IX, pt. 2, p. 240.

[69] *Ibid.*

[70] *Ibid.*, p. 239.

[71] William L. Mathieson, *British Slavery and Its Abolition*, 1823–1838 (London, 1926), pp. 10–11.

[72] Agreement with Thomas Hollingsworth, London, February, 1813, Misc. Un. Docs. (L.C. film), XIII, p. 13.

[73] Clearances of Society's estates, Misc. Un. Docs. (L.C. film), IX, pt. 2, pp. 239–240.

[74] Accounts for 1818, Misc. Un. Docs. (L.C. film), XII, pp. 261–273.

[75] *Ibid.*

[76] *Ibid.*, XII, p. 262.

[77] Lowell Joseph Ragatz, *Statistics for the Study of British Caribbean Economic History, 1763–1833* (London, 1928), Table III, p. 8; Forster Clarke to Bishop of Barbados, Barbados, July 28, 1834, Misc. Un. Docs. (L.C. film), VIII, p. 195; Plantation accounts for 1813, *ibid.*, X, pp. 29–32.

NOTES TO CHAPTER IV

OF THE PRODUCE OF THE PLANTATIONS

[1] Memorandum of May 16, 1733, Fulham Palace MSS (L.C. Trans.), "Barbadoes," No. 71.

[2] Report on condition of the estates, July 11, 1761, Misc. Un. Docs. (L.C. film), IX, pt. I, pp. 346–353.

[3] John Davy, *The West Indies before and since Slave Emancipation, comprising the Windward and Leeward Islands' Military Command: Founded on Notes and Observations Collected during a Three Years' Residence* (London, 1854), p. 52.

[4] H. C. Prinsen Geerligs, *The World's Cane Sugar Industry, Past and Present* (Manchester, 1912), p. 4.

[5] Richard Ligon, *A True and Exact History of the Island of Barbados* (London, 1657), p. 85.

[6] "The Time & Season of Planting & Reaping Sugar Canes as given by Coll. Cleland, October 27, 1711," Misc. Un. Docs. (L.C. film), XIII, pp. 248–249.

[7] John Ashley to the Bishop of London [August, 1733], Fulham Palace MSS (L.C. Trans.), "Barbadoes," No. 47. Ashley added, "I have wrote at large to Mr. Walpole thereupon, and heartily wish our worthy patriots may take our case into consideration."

[8] Bryan Edwards, *The History, Civil and Commercial, of the British Colonies in the West Indies*, 2 vols. (London, 1794), II, p. 244.

[9] Abstract of S.P.G. Proceedings, printed with Annual *Sermon*, 1712, pp. 36–38.

[10] Charles Cunningham to S.P.G. Secretary, Barbados, September 20, 1717, Fulham Palace MSS (L.C. Trans.), "Barbadoes," No. 104.

[11] Attorneys to S.P.G. Secretary, Barbados, July 10, 1761, Misc. Un. Docs. (L.C. film), IX, pt. 1, p. 348.

[12] Typical invoices are: John Smalridge's for July 20, 1725, Misc. Un. Docs. (L.C. film), IX, pt. 1, pp. 80–81; invoice for goods shipped to Codrington College, October 31, 1813, *ibid.*, XIII, pp. 194–196. A good inventory of the plantations is that for July 25, 1805, Misc. Un. Docs. (L.C. film), XIII, pp. 103–106.

[13] Otis Paul Starkey, *The Economic Geography of Barbados; a Study of the Relationship between Environmental Variations and Economic Development* (New York, 1939), p. 36.

[14] John Smalridge to George Smalridge, Barbados, March 23, 1711, S.P.G. MSS (L.C. Trans.), A 6, p. 213.

[15] S.P.G. Attorneys to S.P.G. Secretary, Barbados, May 13, 1779, S.P.G. MSS (L.C. Trans.), B 6, Pt. 1, p. 461.

[16] George R. Porter, *The Nature and Properties of the Sugar Cane,* quoted by Starkey, *op. cit.,* p. 37.

[17] James Grainger, "Song of the Cane Fields," *Sugar Cane, Song of the Cane Fields.* Quoted in *De Bow's Review,* IX (1850), p. 243, as taken from the Whittingham printing, 1822, of One Hundred Volumes of British Poets.

[18] "The Time and Season of Planting and Reaping Sugar Canes ... Oct. 27, 1711," Misc. Un. Docs. (L.C. film), XIII, pp. 248–249.

[19] *Ibid.*

[20] Edwards, *op. cit.,* II, p. 211.

[21] John Smalridge to S.P.G. Secretary, Barbados, July 20, 1725, in Misc. Un. Docs. (L.C. film), IX, pt. 1, p. 66.

[22] Attorneys to S.P.G. Secretary, Barbados, June 20, 1748, Misc. Un. Docs. (L.C. film), IX, pt. 1, pp. 181–192. Griffith Hughes, *The Natural History of Barbados* (London, 1750), pp. 244–252.

[23] Bishop of St. Asaph to Archbishop of Canterbury, London, February 29, 1760, Lambeth Palace MSS (L.C. Trans.), 1123, pt. 2, No. 168.

[24] Edwards, *op. cit.,* II, p. 241.

[25] Edward Clarke to S.P.G. Secretary, Barbados, June 29, 1796, Misc. Un. Docs. (L.C. film), XIII, p. 69.

[26] Attorneys to S.P.G. Secretary, Barbados, August 28, 1776, S.P.G. MSS. (L.C. Trans.), B 6, Pt. 1, pp. 455–456.

[27] John Smalridge to S.P.G. Secretary, Barbados, July 28, 1782, Misc. Un. Docs. (L.C. film), X, pt. 1, pp. 4–5.

[28] *Ibid.,* October 12, 1724, *ibid.,* IX, pt. 1, p. 4.

[29] *Ibid.,* July 20, 1725, *ibid.,* p. 67.

[30] *Ibid.,* September 1, 1725, *ibid.,* pp. 68–71.

[31] Thomas Rotherham to S.P.G. Secretary, Barbados, December 7, 1746, Misc. Un. Docs. (L.C. film), IX, pt. 2, pp. 230–236. John Payne to S.P.G. Secretary, Barbados, August 5, 1747, Misc. Un. Docs. (L.C. film), IX, pt. 1, p. 132.

[32] Starkey, *op. cit.,* pp. 78–79, 90–91, 103–104, 128.

[33] Hughes, *op. cit.,* p. 245. Edwards defined the blast as "the *aphis* of Linnaeus" (*op. cit.,* II, p. 214).

[34] Abstract of S.P.G. Proceedings, printed with Annual *Sermon,* 1736, pp. 52–54.

[35] John Payne to S.P.G. Secretary, Barbados, August 5, 1747, Misc. Un. Docs., (L.C. film), IX, pt. 1, p. 132.

[36] John Smalridge, Observations on the changes made by Charles Cunningham, Barbados, *circa* 1718, Misc. Un. Docs. (L.C. film), IX, pt. 1, pp. 142–153.

[37] Edward Clarke to S.P.G. Secretary, Barbados, August 23, 1798, Misc. Un. Docs. (L.C. film), XIII, p. 83.

[38] Charles Bolton to Bishop of London, Barbados, May 30, 1732, Fulham Palace MSS (L.C. Trans.), "Barbados," No. 100. Bolton made his profit by selling to the Society the casks for its rum and also by buying from the Society at low prices and selling when the market was high.

[39] Meeting of the Attorneys, Barbados, September 18, 1755, summarized in S.P.G. Journal (L.C. Photo), Vol. 13, pp. 85–96.

[40] Edward Clarke to S.P.G. Secretary, Barbados, June 22, 1798, Misc. Un. Docs. (L.C. film), XIII, pp. 77–78.

[41] Anonymous, "Observations on improvement in Distilling," from the Barbados *Gazette,* Saturday, October 22, 1737, *Caribbeana,* II, p. 244.

[42] Report of Conrade Pile, Accountant to the Society, Misc. Un. Docs. (L.C. film), IX, pt. 2, pp. 239–242.

[43] William Bryant to S.P.G. Secretary, Plymouth, October 7, 1746, Misc. Un. Docs. (L.C. film), IX, pt. 2, pp. 221–224.

[44] Thomas Falcon to S.P.G. Secretary, Barbados, May 18, 1759, summarized in S.P.G. Journal (L.C. Photo), Vol. 14, pp. 173–183.

[45] Frank Wesley Pitman, *The Development of the British West Indies, 1700–1763* (New Haven, 1917), p. 134. "A letter from a Gentlemen in Town to his Friend in the Country," from the Barbados *Gazette*, May 15, 1734, *Caribbeana*, I, p. 328.

[46] Account of the sale of 20 hhds of sugar by Marmaduke Trattle, September, 1822, Misc. Un. Docs. (L.C. film), IX, pt. 2, p. 45.

[47] Draft of a letter by the Bishop of St. Asaph, Robert Drummond, to the Attorneys, London, March 15, 1760, Lambeth Palace MSS (L.C. Trans.), 1123, pt. 2, No. 172.

[48] Clearances of Society's estates, Misc. Un. Docs. (L.C. film), IX, pt. 2, pp. 239–242.

[49] Compiled from "The Barbadoes Account" printed each year with the Annual *Sermon*, except as noted in brackets.

[50] Pitman, *op. cit.*, facing p. 98.

[51] Plantation Accounts for 1725, in Misc. Un. Docs. (L.C. film), XII, pp. 99–131.

[52] John Smalridge to S.P.G. Secretary, Barbados, October 12, 1724, Misc. Un. Docs. (L.C. film), IX, pt. 1, p. 4.

[53] *Ibid.*, June 20, 1724, *ibid.*, pp. 17–19.

[54] *Ibid.*, July 25, 1724, *ibid.*, pp. 15–16.

[55] Anonymous, "Some Thoughts on Exchange," from the Barbados *Gazette*, January 21, 1735, *Caribbeana*, II, p. 119.

[56] Anonymous, "On the Sugar Trade," *ibid.*, II, p. 37.

[57] Starkey, *op. cit.*, pp. 92–93.

[58] Clearances of the Society's Estate in Barbados from 1750, Misc. Un. Docs. (L.C. film), IX, pt. 2, pp. 239–242.

[59] Starkey, *op. cit.*, facing p. 103.

[60] Thomas Rotherham to S.P.G. Secretary, Barbados, May 10, 1753, Misc. Un. Docs. (L.C. film), IX, pt. 1, pp. 309–311.

[61] On March 10, 1757, the Society wrote Rotheram that the French ships had chased the sugar ships, which doubtless was the reason that the 1775 accounts had not yet reached London. See Misc. Un. Docs. (L.C. film), IX, pt. 1, p. 343.

[62] Codrington Attorneys to S.P.G. Secretary, Barbados, July 10, 1760, Misc. Un. Docs. (L.C. film), IX, pt. 2, pp. 144–149.

[63] James Butcher to S.P.G. Secretary, Barbados, June 2, 1773, S.P.G. MSS (L.C. Trans.), B 6, pt. 1, p. 340. Sir John Gay Alleyne to S.P.G. Secretary, Barbados, April 23, 1774, S.P.G. MSS (L.C. Trans.), B 6, pt. 1, pp. 372–378.

[64] Minutes of S.P.G. Attorneys, Barbados, January 30, 1776, S.P.G. MSS (L.C. Trans.), B 6, pt. 1, pp. 449–450. Ragatz, *op. cit.*, pp. 8–11. Starkey, *op. cit.*, p. 110.

[65] Minutes of S.P.G. Attorneys, Barbados, October 6 and 7, 1777, Misc. Un. Docs. (L.C. film), XIII, pp. 20–25. Attorneys to S.P.G. Secretary, Barbados, May 13, 1779, S.P.G. MSS (L.C. Trans.), B 6, pt. 1, pp. 461–465. Abstract of S.P.G. Proceedings, printed with Annual *Sermon*, 1781, pp. 45–47.

[66] Clearance of the Society's estate in Barbados, 1750–1823, Misc. Un. Docs. (L.C. film), IX, pt. 2, p. 239.

[67] Starkey, *op. cit.*, pp. 107–112.

[68] Clearances of the Society's Estate in Barbados from 1750 to 1823, Misc. Un. Docs. (L.C. film), IX, pt. 2, p. 239.

[69] Mathieson, *op. cit.*, pp. 9–10.

[70] Edward Clarke to John Braithwaite, Barbados, September 18, 1797, Misc. Un. Docs. (L.C. film), XIII, p. 74.

[71] Clearances of the Society's Estate in Barbados from 1750 to 1823, Misc. Un. Docs. (L.C. film), IX, pt. 2, pp. 239–242.

NOTES TO CHAPTER V

OF THE NEGROES THEREON

[1] Klingberg, *Anglican Humanitarianism*, p. 185.

[2] *Idem*, "British Humanitarianism at Codrington," pp. 451–486.

[3] William Fleetwood, *A Sermon Preached before the Society* (London, 1711).

[4] C. S. S. Higham, "The Negro Policy of Christopher Codrington," *Journal of Negro History*, X (1925), pp. 150–153.

[5] Klingberg, "British Humanitarianism at Codrington," pp. 454–455.

[6] See the refutation of this view by the Rev. Thomas Wharton and the attorneys in S.P.G. MSS (L.C. Trans.), A 26, pp. 23–24; *ibid.*, B 6, pt. 1, pp. 287–293, 433–437. As is shown in Chapter VI of this work, the idea that the college was for the liberal education of the whites came to prevail during the eighteenth century, despite the founder's intentions.

[7] William Johnson to S.P.G. Secretary, Barbados, January 14, 1737, S.P.G. MSS (L.C. Trans.), A 26, pp. 385–389.

[8] Klingberg, *Anglican Humanitarianism*, p. 21.

[9] Arthur Holt to the Bishop of London, Barbados, December 21, 1727, Fulham Palace MSS (L.C. Trans.), "Barbadoes," No. 128.

[10] The Bishop of London was called upon to arrange with the Admiralty to transport the couple, together with a servant, on board the *Speedwell*, or some other man-of-war bound for Barbados. See Dr. Hans Sloane to S.P.G. Secretary, London, March 4, 1713, S.P.G. MSS (L.C. Trans.), A 8, pp. 19–21; Dr. Gideon Harvey to same, London, March 20, 1713, *ibid.*, pp. 22–23; Society Cursitors Office to Bishop of London, February 28, 1713, *ibid.*, p. 107.

[11] Starkey, *op. cit.*, pp. 70–71.

[12] A. Caldecott, *The Church in the West Indies* (London, 1898), p. 62.

[13] Abstract of S.P.G. Proceedings, printed with Annual *Sermon*, 1715, pp. 49–50; Draft of a bill in S.P.G. MSS (L.C. Trans.), B 6, pt. 1, pp. 478–482.

[14] David Humphreys, *An Historical Account of the Incorporated Society for the Propagation of the Gospel in Foregn Parts* (London, 1730), pp. 231–249.

[15] Abstract of S.P.G. Proceedings, printed with Annual *Sermon*, 1741, pp. 68–69. For an account of the Charleston Negro School, begun in 1740, see Klingberg, *An Appraisal of the Negro in Colonial South Carolina*, pp. 101–122.

[16] Draft of a proclamation in S.P.G. MSS (L.C. Trans.), B 6, pt. 1, pp. 478–482.

[17] William Johnson to S.P.G. Secretary, Barbados, January 14, 1737, S.P.G. MSS (L.C. Trans.), A 26, pp. 385–389.

[18] Abstract of S.P.G. Proceedings, printed with Annual *Sermon*, 1715, pp. 52–60.

[19] Mr. Holt was charged with lack of sobriety, immorality, levity, heterodoxy, offensive conversation, and irregular living. But the fact that there was some disagreement on that score is evidenced by certificates of his good character, signed by about 120 citizens of Barbados. See Misc. Un. Docs. (L.C. film), I 4, pp. 88–92. It is also interesting to note that he was the father of Arthur Holt who later became one of the Society's most trusted attorneys.

[20] Copy of testimonial, Barbados, 1715, Misc. Un. Docs. (L.C. film), I 4, pp. 89–90; Certificate by George Waldron and others, Barbados, January, 1715, *ibid.*, pp. 91–92.

[21] Charles Cunningham to S.P.G., Barbados, September 20, 1717, Fulham Palace MSS (L.C. Trans.), "Barbadoes," No. 104.

[22] Abstract of S.P.G. Proceedings, printed with Annual *Sermon*, 1715, p. 57.

[23] Minutes of S.P.G. Meeting, January 15, 1725, S.P.G. Journals (L.C. film), Vol. 5, pp. 25–30.

[24] Thomas Wilkie to the Bishop of London, Barbados, March 7, 1727, Fulham Palace MSS (L.C. Trans.), "Barbadoes," No. 127. Wilkie's appointment as catechist was announced in the Abstract of S.P.G. Proceedings, printed with Annual *Sermon*, 1727, pp. 42–43.

[25] Arthur Holt to S.P.G. Secretary, Barbados, April 3, 1732, S.P.G. MSS (L.C. Trans.), A 24, pp. 201–206.

[26] Abstract of S.P.G. Proceedings, printed with Annual *Sermons*, 1712 to 1767. See also "Extracts from Barbados Journal giving the History of Codrington College, 1710–1813," Misc. Un. Docs. (L.C. film), XIII, pp. 215–221.

[27] Abstract of S.P.G. Proceedings, printed with Annual *Sermon*, 1713, p. 49, and *ibid.*, 1715, p. 57.

[28] Arthur Holt to S.P.G. Secretary, Barbados, April 3, 1732, S.P.G. MSS (L.C. Trans.), A 24, pp. 201–206; same to Bishop of London, Barbados, May 2, 1733, Fulham Palace MSS (L.C. Trans.), "Barbadoes," No. 70.

[29] William Johnson to Bishop of London, Barbados, June 2, 1733, Fulham Palace MSS (L.C. Trans.), "Barbadoes," No. 30.

[30] Attorneys to S.P.G. Secretary, Barbados, June 5, 1776, Misc. Un. Docs. (L.C. film), XIII, pp. 180–183; James Butcher to same, Barbados, August 30, 1768, S.P.G. MSS (L.C. Trans.), B 6, pt. 1, pp. 275–279.

[31] Henry Worsley to Bishop of London, Barbados, March 17, 1727, Fulham Palace MSS (L.C. Trans.), "Barbadoes," No. 112.

[32] Abstract of S.P.G. Proceedings, printed with Annual *Sermon*, 1715, p. 57.

[33] James Butcher to S.P.G. Secretary, Barbados, July 25, 1774, S.P.G. MSS (L.C. Trans.), B 6, pt. 1, 389–393; Michael Mashart to S.P.G. Secretary, Barbados, August 12, 1774, *ibid.*, pp. 404–408.

[34] Thomas Wilkie to Bishop of London, Barbados, March 7, 1727, Fulham Palace MSS (L.C. Trans.), "Barbadoes," No. 127.

[35] *Ibid.*

[36] *Ibid.*

[37] David Humphreys to John Smalridge, London, January 17, 1729, Misc. Un. Docs. (L.C. film), XIII, pp. 47–49.

[38] Abstract of S.P.G. Proceedings, printed with Annual *Sermon*, 1713, p. 51.

[39] *Ibid.*, 1728, p. 41. See above, n. 37.

[40] Minutes of Attorneys, Barbados, September 12, 1728, Misc. Un. Docs. (L.C. film), XII, pp. 205–207.

[41] Sampson Smirk to S.P.G. Secretary, Barbados, September 5, 1740, S.P.G. MSS (L.C. Trans.), B 8, p. 72; same to same, Barbados, April 16, 1741, pp. 115–116.

[42] Abel Alleyne to S.P.G. Secretary, Barbados, July 18, 1741, S.P.G. MSS (L.C. Trans.), B 8, p. 101; same to same, Barbados, September 11, 1741, *ibid.*, p. 106; same to same, Barbados, December 9, 1741, *ibid.*, pp. 109–110.

[43] Philip Bearcroft to Abel Alleyne, London, December 31, 1741, S.P.G. MSS (L.C. Trans.), B 8, pp. 199–204; same to Sampson Smirk, London, December 31, 1741, *ibid.*, pp. 205–206.

[44] Joseph Bewsher to S.P.G. Secretary, Barbados, October 5, 1745, Misc. Un. Docs. (L.C. film), IX, pt. 1, pp. 354–359.

[45] John Pinder to S.P.G. Secretary, Barbados, January 22, 1819, Misc. Un. Docs. (L.C. film), VIII, pp. 231–234.

[46] Beilby Porteus, *A Sermon Preached before the Society* ... (London, 1783), p. 20.

[47] Arthur Holt to Bishop of London, Barbados, December 21, 1727, Fulham Palace MSS (L.C. Trans.), "Barbadoes," No. 128.

[48] Arthur Holt to Bishop of London, Barbados, April 30, 1725, Fulham Palace MSS (L.C. Trans.), "Barbadoes," No. 2.

[49] William Johnson to S.P.G. Secretary, Barbados, January 14, 1737, S.P.G. MSS (L.C. Trans.), A 26, pp. 385–389; and Annual *Sermons* of 1711, 1740, 1741, and 1754.

[50] Abstract of S.P.G. Proceedings, printed with Annual *Sermon*, 1715, pp. 49–50.

[51] William Johnson to S.P.G. Secretary, Barbados, January 14, 1737, S.P.G. MSS (L.C. Trans.), A 26, pp. 385–389.

[52] Joseph Bewsher to S.P.G. Secretary, Barbados, October 5, 1745, Misc. Un. Docs. (L.C. film), IX, pt. 1, pp. 354–359.

[53] Michael Mashart to S.P.G. Secretary, Barbados, June 15, 1775, S.P.G. MSS (L.C. Trans.), B 6, pt. 1, pp. 423–427.

[54] Joseph Bewsher to S.P.G. Secretary, Barbados, October 5, 1745, Misc. Un. Docs. (L.C. film), IX, pt. 1, pp. 354–359.

[55] Abstract of S.P.G. Proceedings, printed with Annual *Sermon*, 1716, p. 17.

[56] Abel Alleyne to S.P.G. Secretary, Barbados, July 18, 1741, S.P.G. MSS (L.C. Trans.), B 8, pp. 99–104.

[57] Joseph Bewsher to S.P.G. Secretary, Barbados, October 5, 1745, Misc. Un. Docs. (L.C. film), IX, pt. 1, pp. 354–359.

[58] S.P.G. MSS (L.C. Trans.), B 8, pp. 120–121.

[59] Joseph Bewsher to S.P.G. Secretary, Barbados, October 5, 1745, Misc. Un. Docs. (L.C. film), IX, pt. 1, pp. 354–359.

[60] James Butcher to S.P.G. Secretary, Barbados, May 4, 1769, S.P.G. MSS (L.C. Trans.), B 6, pt. 1, pp. 305–307.

[61] William Johnson to S.P.G. Secretary, Barbados, January 14, 1737, S.P.G. MSS (L.C. Trans.), A 26, pp. 385–389.

[62] Thomas Wharton to S.P.G. Secretary, Barbados, August 30, 1768, S.P.G. MSS (L.C. Trans.), B 6, pt. 1, pp. 287–293.

[63] John H. Pinder, "Regulations ..." to S.P.G. Secretary, Barbados [1819], Misc. Un. Docs. (L.C. film), XIII, p. 232.

[64] Minutes of Meeting of college building commissioners, Barbados, September 7, 1714, Misc. Un. Docs. (L.C. film), I 4, pp. 79–81.

[65] Grand Inquest to Robert Lowther, Barbados, December 9–12, 1718, Fulham Palace MSS (L.C. Trans.), "Barbadoes," No. 1.

[66] Charles Cunningham to S.P.G. Secretary, Barbados, September 20, 1717, Fulham Palace MSS (L.C. film), "Barbadoes," No. 104.

[67] Arthur Holt to Bishop of London, Barbados, March 7, 1729, Fulham Palace MSS (L.C. film), "Barbadoes," No. 119.

[68] Attorneys to S.P.G. Secretary, Barbados, July 11, 1761, Misc. Un. Docs. (L.C. film), IX, pt. 1, pp. 346–353; John Hodgson to S.P.G. Secretary, Barbados, July 17, 1760, as abstracted in S.P.G. Journals (L.C. film), Vol. 15, pp. 17–40.

[69] James Butcher to S.P.G. Secretary, Barbados, August 30, 1768, S.P.G. MSS (L.C. Trans.), B 6, pt. 1, pp. 275–280.

[70] *Ibid.*, Barbados, May 4, 1769, in S.P.G. MSS (L.C. Trans.), B 6, pt. 1, pp. 305–307.

[71] Minutes of Attorneys, Barbados, June 29, 1775, S.P.G. MSS (L.C. Trans.), B 6, pt. 1, pp. 428–430.

[72] Michael Mashart to Daniel Burton, Barbados, June 2, 1771, S.P.G. MSS (L.C. Trans.), B 6, pt. 1, pp. 308–309; same to same, Barbados, July 30, 1772, *ibid.*, pp. 334–335.

[73] Attorneys to S.P.G. Secretary, Barbados, September 14, 1775, S.P.G. MSS (L.C. Trans.), B 6, pt. 1, pp. 433–437.

[74] Thomas Wharton to S.P.G. Secretary, Barbados, August 30, 1768, S.P.G. MSS (L.C. Trans.), B 6, pt. 1, pp. 287–293.

[75] Joseph Bewsher to S.P.G. Secretary, Barbados, October 5, 1745, Misc. Un. Docs. (L.C. film), IX, pt. 1, pp. 354–359.

[76] Arthur Holt to Bishop of London, Barbados, December 21, 1727, Fulham Palace MSS (L.C. Trans.), "Barbadoes," No. 128.

[77] Barbados Clergy to Bishop of London, Barbados, September 25, 1788, Fulham Palace MSS (L.C. Trans.), "Barbadoes," No. 154.

[78] Abel Clinckett to Bishop of Barbados, December 22, 1827, Fulham Palace MSS (L.C. Trans.), "Barbadoes," No. 157.

[79] Abstract of S.P.G. Proceedings, printed with Annual *Sermon*, 1798, pp. 48–49; Klingberg, "British Humanitarianism at Codrington," p. 477.

[80] Klingberg, "British Humanitarianism at Codrington," pp. 464–477.

[81] Edward Clarke to S.P.G. Secretary, Barbados, April 25, 1799, Misc. Un. Docs. (L.C. film), XIII, pp. 92–94.

[82] Edward Clarke to S.P.G. Secretary, Barbados, April 25, 1799, Misc. Un. Docs. (L.C. film), XIII, p. 94.

[83] Forster Clarke to Bishop of London, Barbados, June 28, 1824, Fulham Palace MSS (L.C. Trans.), "Barbadoes," No. 158.

[84] Bishop of Barbados to S.P.G. Secretary, Barbados, October 28, 1829, Misc. Un. Docs. (L.C. film), XIII, pp. 239–244. Meeting of Barbados Committee, London, February 8, 1825, Misc. Un. Docs. (L.C. film), XIII, pp. 223–226; Regulations, 1819, *ibid.*, pp. 231–238.

[85] The unmarried state of many of the Negroes throughout the colonial world was the concern of many of the Society's missionaries who urged the right of the slaves to the sacrament of marriage as well as of baptism. See Klingberg, *Anglican Humanitarianism* and *Negro in Colonial South Carolina, passim.*

[86] Meeting of Barbados Committee, London House, February 8, 1825, Misc. Un. Docs. (L.C. film), XIII, pp. 223–226.

[87] Bishop of Barbados to Bishop of London, Barbados, October 1, 1829, Fulham Palace MSS (L.C. Trans.), "Barbadoes," No. 162.

[88] Bishop of Barbados to S.P.G. Secretary, Barbados, October 28, 1829, Misc. Un. Docs. (L.C. film), XIII, pp. 239–244. The chapel was "on an eminence over Consetts Bay," and Lord Harewood assisted in the project by furnishing supplies.

⁸⁹ Edward Chandler, *A Sermon Preached before the Society* ... (London, 1719), p. 27.

⁹⁰ William Fleetwood, *A Sermon Preached before the Society* ... (London, 1711), pp. 17–29.

⁹¹ Isaac Maddox, *A Sermon Preached before the Society* ... (London, 1734), p. 28.

⁹² Thomas Secker, *A Sermon Preached before the Society* ... (London, 1741), pp. 7–9. This sermon is also reproduced in Klingberg, *Anglican Humanitarianism*, pp. 213–233.

⁹³ Porteus, *op. cit.*, pp. 3–34.

⁹⁴ Starkey, *op. cit.*, p. 110.

⁹⁵ Porteus, *op. cit.*, p. 17.

⁹⁶ Bishop of Barbados to Bishop of London, Barbados, October 1, 1829, Fulham Palace MSS (L.C. Trans.), "Barbadoes," No. 162.

⁹⁷ Thomas Guyth and Robert Walker, Bodwin, England, July 6, 1831, Misc. Un. Docs. (L.C. film), VIII, p. 228.

⁹⁸ Forster Clarke to Bishop of Barbados, Barbados, July 28, 1834, Misc. Un. Docs. (L.C. film), VIII, pp. 190–195.

⁹⁹ Porteus, *op. cit.*, p. 19.

NOTES TO CHAPTER VI

Of the State and Advancement of the College

¹ Fulham Palace MSS (L.C. Trans.), "Barbadoes," No. 41.

² George Macaulay Trevelyan, *English Social History: A Survey of Six Centuries from Chaucer to Queen Victoria* (New York, 1942), pp. 308–312.

³ Harold T. Wilkins, *Great English Schools* (London, 1925), pp. 261–266.

⁴ A survey of the Barbados parishes, conducted by Bishop Edmund Gibson in 1724, revealed the lack of schools in Barbados in this period. The parish roll call on this subject was as follows: St. Michael's, "no public school but several private schoolmasters"; St. Peter's All Saints, "needs more space for a school"; Christ's Church, "no public school"; St. Lucie's, "none"; St. Phillip's, "several schools"; St. Andrew's, "no school publick or private"; St. Thomas's, "none"; St. George's, "the rooms of a building called the free School decayed long before my time"; St. Joseph's, "none"; and St. James's, "a School where Reading and Writing is Taught, but it is not Endowed." See Fulham Palace MSS (L.C. Trans.), "Barbadoes," No. 179–189.

⁵ Governor Henry Worsley to Bishop of London, Barbados, November 12, 1724, Fulham Palace MSS (L.C. Trans.), "Barbadoes," No. 123.

⁶ Charles Cunningham to the Society, September 20, 1717, Fulham Palace MSS (L.C. Trans.), "Barbadoes," No. 104.

⁷ Arthur Holt to Bishop of London, March 7, 1729, Fulham Palace MSS (L.C. Trans.), "Barbadoes," No. 119.

⁸ Abstract of S.P.G. Proceedings, printed with Annual *Sermon*, 1744, pp. 57–58.

⁹ Pitman, *op. cit.*, p. 3.

¹⁰ Joseph Bewsher to S.P.G. Secretary, October 5, 1745, Misc. Un. Docs. (L.C. film), IX, pt. 1, p. 355; Thomas Rotheram to the Archbishop of Canterbury, Barbados, August 13, 1746, summarized in S.P.G. Journals (L.C. film), Vol. 10, pp. 192–197.

¹¹ The tuition fee was £10 per annum, plus 50 shillings to pay for instruction in writing and arithmetic. There was also a bill of £30 to £40 for food, and £15 "caution money," the last to be paid on entry and returned or accounted for at the end of each year. The only items not listed as supplied were beds and clothing. See Misc. Un. Docs. (L.C. film), IX, pt. 1, p. 119.

¹² The Society had made provision for twenty foundationers, but the Barbados attorneys, who held the administrative power of the school in their hands, had selected seventeen. See Abstract of S.P.G. Proceedings, printed with Annual *Sermon*, 1745, p. 55.

¹³ Thomas Rotheram to S.P.G. Secretary, Barbados, October 7, 1745, Misc. Un. Docs. (L.C. film), IX, pt. 1, p. 361.

¹⁴ Grenville, according to Bewsher, had "great influence" over the Barbadians, and as a "very religious man and a great Lover of Learning," he was able to "rectifie the mistaken notions of some." See Joseph Bewsher to S.P.G. Secretary, Barbados, August 4, 1747, Misc. Un. Docs. (L.C. film), IX, pt. 1, pp. 108–109.

¹⁵ Schoolmasters to S.P.G. Secretary, Barbados, June 20, 1748, Misc. Un. Docs. (L.C. film), IX, pt. 1, pp. 181–189.

¹⁶ Thomas Rotheram to S.P.G. Secretary, Barbados, August 5, 1747, Misc. Un. Docs. (L.C. film), VIII, p. 59; Joseph Bewsher to S.P.G. Secretary, Barbados, August 4, 1747, *ibid.*, 249–252; Minutes of the Attorneys, Barbados, May 26, 1748, *ibid.*, pp. 26–31.

¹⁷ Abstract of S.P.G. Proceedings, printed with Annual *Sermon*, 1745, p. 55.

¹⁸ Bryant had been trained at St. John's, Cambridge, and Cattel had received his training at St. Thomas' Hospital, London; abstract of S.P.G. Proceedings, printed with Annual *Sermon*, 1748, p. 67.

¹⁹ After the death of Bryant in 1750, the people of Barbados demanded a successor in mathematics. See Thomas Rotheram to S.P.G. Secretary, Barbados, May 10, 1753, Misc. Un. Docs. (L.C. film), IX, pt. 1, p. 311; Trevelyan, *op. cit.*, 183–366. Thomas Rotheram to S.P.G. Secretary, Barbados, December 30, 1747, Misc. Un. Docs. (L.C. film), IX, pt. 1, pp. 134–135.

²⁰ Meeting of Codrington Attorneys, Barbados, June 10, 1748, Misc. Un. Docs. (L.C. film), IX, pt. 1, p. 119.

²¹ Printed advertisement, Barbados, May 6, 1748, Misc. Un. Docs. (L.C. film), IX, pt. 1, pp. 118–119; Meeting of Codrington Attorneys, Barbados, July 4, 1748, Misc. Un. Docs. (L.C. film), IX, pt. 1, p. 121. Admitted by unanimous agreement were:

Joseph Lee, Son of Joseph and Mary Lee, both October 31st 1736. His father was by trade a Silver Smith late of good reputation in the Island, who had kept his Son in the School ever since it was first opened at his own expence, where he had made a considerable progress but being lately dead, & his Mother left with a large family, She was not able to pay for his learning any longer and therefore must have taken him away if he had been excluded from the foundation.

Richard Downes, Son of Rich'd Downes, born Sept. 11th, 1739, apparently a Boy of very good parts and reads well.

Reynolds Williams, Son of Tho. Williams, born October 1736 of full age, but otherwise apparently a very fine Boy.

John Payne, Son of John Payne, the Society's Overseer, born 30 Jan. 1738.

John Hall, Son of Thomas Hall, Carpenter, born December 22, 1737.

Melchior Garner, Son of Nicholas Garner born Aug't 22, 1737.

²² Printed advertisement, Barbados, May 6, 1748, Misc. Un. Docs. (L.C. film), IX, pt. 1, pp. 118–119.

²³ Thomas Rotheram to S.P.G. Secretary, Barbados, October 7, 1745, Misc. Un. Docs. (L.C. film), IX, pt. 1, pp. 360–363; Rules for scholars, Misc. Un. Docs. (L.C. film), VIII, pp. 9–10.

[24] Thomas Rotheram to S.P.G. Secretary, Barbados, October 7, 1745, Misc. Un. Docs. (L.C. film), IX, pt. 1, p. 362.

[25] *Ibid.*

[26] *Ibid.*, August 5, 1747, Misc. Un. Docs. (L.C. film), IX, pt. 1, pp. 139–141.

[27] William Cattel to S.P.G. Secretary, Barbados, June 27, 1748, Misc. Un. Docs. (L.C. film), IX, pt. 1, pp. 113–114; Joseph Bewsher to S.P.G. Secretary, Barbados, June 24, 1748, Misc. Un. Docs. (L.C. film), IX, pt. 1, pp. 110–112.

[28] Thomas Rotheram to S.P.G. Secretary, Barbados, March 8, 1748, Misc. Un. Docs. (L.C. film), IX, pt. 1, p. 265.

[29] Received by William Bryant from J. Bird, London, April 17, 1746, Misc. Un. Docs. (L.C. film), VIII, p. 4; account with James Mann and James Asycough, April 14, 1746, Misc. Un. Docs. (L.C. film), IX, pt. 1, p. 316.

[30] Abstracts of S.P.G. Proceedings, printed with Annual *Sermons,* 1712–1716; Extracts from the Barbados Journal, Misc. Un. Docs. (L.C. film), XIII, pp. 215–222.

[31] Journal of S.P.G. (L.C. film), Vol. 10, p. 285–304.

[32] Codrington Attorneys to S.P.G. Secretary, Barbados, May 28, 1762, S.P.G. MSS (L.C. Trans.), B 6, pt. 1, pp. 244–251.

[33] Nathan Treadway, a boy from Christ Church Hospital was sent to Codrington to teach "the boys upon the foundation in writing and arithmetick at a salary of £30." See Thomas Rotheram to S.P.G. Secretary, Barbados, August 5, 1747, Misc. Un. Docs. (L.C. film), VIII, pp. 57–60. Thomas Barnard and Thomas Rotheram to S.P.G. Secretary, Barbados, August 24, 1750, Misc. Un. Docs. (L.C. film), IX, pt. 1, 251–252; William Cattel to S.P.G. Secretary, Barbados, July 7, 1753, *ibid.*, pp. 314–315; George Fothergill to S.P.G. Secretary, Oxford, March 13, 1753, *ibid.*, pp. 325–326; same to same, Oxford, April 25, 1753, *ibid.*, pp. 312–313; Minutes of S.P.G. meeting, London, May 18, 1753, S.P.G. Journals (L.C. film), Vol. 12, pp. 253–260.

[34] Prepared principally from Pascoe, *op. cit.*, II, p. 783.

[35] S.P.G. Journals (L.C. film), Vol. 15, pp. 161–179, 248–273; *ibid.*, Vol. 16, pp. 287–322.

[36] Attorneys to S.P.G. Secretary, Barbados, May 28, 1762, S.P.G. MSS (L.C. Trans.), B 6, pt. 1, pp. 244–251; Abstract of S.P.G. Proceedings, printed with Annual *Sermon,* 1764, p. 106; *ibid.*, 1763, p. 88.

[37] James Butcher to S.P.G. Secretary, Barbados, August 30, 1768, S.P.G. MSS (L.C. Trans.), B 6, pt. 1, pp. 275–280.

[38] Rules to be Observed by all Scholars, July 5, 1766, S.P.G. MSS (L.C. Trans.), B 6, pt. 1, pp. 270–273.

[39] David Davies to S.P.G. Secretary, September 15, 1765, Misc. Un. Docs. (L.C. film), XIII, pp. 53–55; Minutes of S.P.G. meeting, September 19, 1766, S.P.G. Journals (L.C. film), Vol. 17, pp. 109–148.

[40] Sir John Alleyne to S.P.G. Secretary, Barbados, August 16, 1773, S.P.G. MSS (L.C. Trans.), B 6, pt. 1, p. 356.

[41] Attorneys to S.P.G. Secretary, Barbados, September 14, 1775, S.P.G. MSS (L.C. Trans.), B 6, pt. 1, p. 433; James Butcher to S.P.G. Secretary, Barbados, August 30, 1768, S.P.G. MSS (L.C. Trans.), B 6, pt. 1, pp. 275–280; same to same, Barbados, June 2, 1773, *ibid.*, pp. 339–341; same to same, Barbados, July 25, 1774, *ibid.*, pp. 389–393; same to same, Barbados, August 6, 1774, *ibid.*, pp. 399–403; Michael Mashart to S.P.G. Secretary, Barbados, August 12, 1774, *ibid.*, pp. 404–408; minutes of meeting of Codrington Attorneys, Barbados, June 29, 1775, *ibid.*, pp. 428–430.

[42] Abstract of S.P.G. Proceedings, printed with Annual *Sermon*, 1789, p. 40; Extracts from the Barbados Journal, Misc. Un. Docs. (L.C. film), XIII, pp. 215–222.

[43] Extracts from the Barbados Journal, Misc. Un. Docs. (L.C. film), XIII, p. 220.

[44] *Ibid.*, p. 221; T. Herbert Bindley, *Annals of Codrington College, Barbados, 1710–1910* (London, 1910), pp. 25–26.

[45] Extracts from the Barbados Journal, Misc. Un. Docs. (L.C. film), XIII, p. 220.

[46] Bindley, *op. cit.*, p. 56.

[47] Richard Rawle, Account of Codrington College, June 2, 1847, Misc. Un. Docs. (L.C. film), IX, pt. 2, pp. 195–197; Extracts from the Barbados Journal, Misc. Un. Docs. (L.C. film), XIII, pp. 215–222.

[48] *Ibid.*

[49] Pascoe, *op. cit.*, I, 200b.

[50] Bindley, *op. cit.*, p. 28.

[51] Under Bishop Coleridge's guidance, a large institution, promoted by Lord Combermere and "liberally seconded" by the legislature, was providing for about 160 white children who were being educated "precisely upon the plan of the national schools in England. . . ." A large school for colored children, also in Bridgetown, had been placed by its Negro managers under the Bishop's superintendence. Further, a boarding school entirely for girls and four more schools for both boys and girls had been opened by this "indefatigable bishop." See Henry Nelson Coleridge, *Six Months in the West Indies in 1825* (London, 1826), pp. 50–51.

[52] Bishop of Barbados to Bishop of London, April 27, 1825, Fulham Palace MSS (L.C. Trans.), "Barbadoes," No. 157.

[53] Coleridge, *op. cit.*, p. 54 n.

[54] Bishop of Barbados to S.P.G. Secretary, Barbados, July 31, 1829, Misc. Un. Docs. (L.C. film), VIII, pp. 101–104. As for the three older boys, Bishop Coleridge commented that their spelling and their translations "would almost disgrace a very little boy." The Rev. Edward Eliot, archdeacon of Barbados, had "very properly" given the boys the examination in Latin, and the Bishop forwarded translations from Caesar to illustrate his point. The new schoolmaster, the Rev. John Packer was, however, proceeding to "ground" the boys as best he could, and improvement would shortly be expected.

[55] Meeting of College Council, Barbados, September 1, 1829, Misc. Un. Docs. (L.C. film), VIII, pp. 123–124. Present were the Bishop; John Hothersall Pinder, the principal; E. Parris Smith, the tutor; and John Packer, the master of the grammar school, which was not closed with the establishment of the college.

[56] John H. Pinder to S.P.G. Secretary, Barbados, July 14, 1830, Misc. Un. Docs. (L.C. film), VIII, pp. 257–261.

[57] Pascoe, *op. cit.*, II, p. 782; Bindley, *op. cit.*, p. 33.

[58] Reports of Principal and Tutor of Codrington College, Barbados, July 14, 1830, Misc. Un. Docs. (L.C. film), VIII, 257–264. Lecture hours were from twelve to two. The subject of the lectures being addressed to all classes during the first hour on Monday, Tuesday, and Wednesday was "The Ecclesiastical History of England from the commencement of the 16th Century to the period of the Restoration." The junior class had completed the first book of Homer's *Iliad*, and the first book of Cicero's *De Officiis*, and was reading Luke's Gospel.

The senior class had finished the *Oedipus at Colonus* of Sophocles, the first books of the *Historiae* of Tacitus and Euclid, and the Epistles to the Romans and Galatians in the Greek Testament, and had construed the Acts of the Apostles.

[59] Reports of the Principal and Tutor, Barbados, July 14, 1830, Misc. Un. Docs. (L.C. film), VIII, pp. 257–264. The senior class also had work in Hebrew.

[60] Report of Principal of Codrington College, Barbados, July 7, 1834, Misc. Un. Docs. (L.C. film), VIII, pp. 159–162.

[61] As a result of the hurricane damage, and of costs incurred in preparing the college for the reception of academic students, the trust fund which, in 1829, stood at £34,000 was reduced in 1833 to £19,000 and in 1836 to £17,000. With the abolition of slavery, £8,823, 8s. 9d. was received by the Society for Codrington's slaves, but in the next few years expenditure so far exceeded income that the funded capital in 1846 amounted to only £14,725. See Pascoe, *op. cit.*, I, 199 and II, 782.

[62] Pascoe, *op. cit.*, I, pp. 204–205; II, 783, 841.

[63] Caldecott, *op. cit.*, pp. 92, 233.

INDEX

Abbot, Richard, 29

Abolition of slavery, 4; of slave trade, 11, 100; and S.P.G. Negro program, 99; of S.P.G. slaves, 144 n. 61. *See also* Christianization of Negro; Emancipation; Humanitarianism; Reform; Sermons; S.P.G.

Absentee management, 42, 53, 64. *See also* Long-distance management

Abstracts of the Proceedings of S.P.G., 9, 21, 27, 34, 75, 108, 115, circulation, 9; contents (1713), 21; contents (1714), 27; contents (1725), 34

Accounts, financial of Codrington estates, 46, 49, 51, 52, 54, 63, 74; methods of keeping, 75. *See also* Clearances of Codrington estates

Administration of school, 111, 112. *See also* Attorneys; Codrington College; Grammar School; Personnel, School; Schoolmasters

Africa, 85; source of slave labor, 3, 11, 48; slave trade, 101

Agent, Codrington estates in Bridgetown, 45, 48, 73–74, 134 n. 38; functions of, 45. *See also* Bolton, Charles; Town agent

Agriculture. *See* Crop(s); Sugar

Allen, Reynold, sponsor of school, 29

Allen, Thomas, sponsor of school, 29

Alleyne, Abel, manager of Codrington estates, 36, 51, 92, 95, 127 n. 34, 138 nn. 42, 43, 56

Alleyne, Sir John Gay, 57, 116, 132 n. 60, 135 n. 63; 142 n. 40

Allinson, J., assistant schoolmaster, 118

All Souls College, Oxford, 15–16

Anglican Church [Church of England], 3, 11, 86, 116; eighteenth-century position, 5; as institution for reform, 5; Christianity, 91; Anglican ministers as attorneys for Codrington estates, 44

Anglo-American society and humanitarianism, 8

Anglo-French wars, 81

Animals on Codrington estates, 65, 76. *See also* Cattle

Antigua, 16, 29, 88, 100, 120

Antislavery movement, 6, 12. *See also* Abolition; Emancipation; Humanitarianism; Reform; S.P.G.

Ashley, John, 65, 133 n. 7

Assiento Company [Asiento], 51

Asycough, James, 142 n. 29

Attorneys for Codrington estates, 35, 36, 43, 44, 45, 48, 49, 51, 57, 70, 71, 90, 92, 98, 99, 111, 117, 129 nn. 36, 39, 40; 130 nn. 8, 12, 15, 17, 19, 20; 131 nn. 42, 46; 132 nn. 55, 56, 57, 59; 133 nn. 11, 15; 134 nn. 22, 26, 39, 135 nn. 62, 64, 65; 136 nn. 6; 137 nn. 30, 40; 139 nn. 68, 71, 73; 141 nn. 16, 20, 21; 142 nn. 32, 36, 41; Anglican ministers as, 44; charged with working against Negro Christianization, 10, 97, 98; commissions, 74; cost of meetings and entertainment, 35; directed to complete college buildings, 36; disagreement among, 50–53; hamper progress of college, 35, 37; inquiry into condition of estates, 56; meetings, 35, 44; minutes, 44, 45; powers of, 44; recommend purchase of another plantation, 56; selection of plantation manager by, 44, 55; sugar growers, 44; trustees, 44

Aylcott, town agent, 73

Baptism of Negroes, 4, 88. *See also* Christianization of Negro

Barbadians, attitude of, 7, 131 n. 33; attitude toward grammar school, 109, 111; and Codrington personnel, 90–91; concern with economic gain, 106; critical of Codrington College project, 35, 84, 103, 109; oppose Negro program at Codrington, 86, 95, 98, 99; planter society, 107; practices of planters, 64–65; rights defended, 77; support college for white education, 96. *See also* Codrington, Christopher; Planters

Ramsay, Gilbert, clergy, attorney for estates, sponsor of school, 29, 50, 125 n. 1, 126 n. 29, 130 n. 1

Raval, Daniel, sponsor of school for St. Christopher's, 29

Rawle, Richard, 143 n. 47

Reading in college program, 117, 118; teacher for Negroes, 95

Receipts for estates, 75. *See also* Clearances; Codrington estates

Reduction of soil's fertility, 66

Reform, 91; eighteenth century, 5; in indifferent society, 85; Parliamentary, 101; slavery, 102

Religion as civilizing influence, 18

Religious education, 88, 94, 95, 97, 98. *See also* Christianization of Negro; S.P.G.

Religious emigration to North America, 18

Rental of Codrington estates, 57, 72, 79–80, 94

Replacement of slaves, 48, 67

Richardson, Samuel, 108

Robertson, Robert, sponsor of school for Nevis, 29

Rock, R. J., Codrington student ordained for Grenada, 120

Rogers, Stephen, St. Philip's, Barbados, 111

Rogers, William, foundation student, 111

Rotheram, John, schoolmaster, 89, 90, 109, 114, 115

Rotheram, Thomas, schoolmaster, 36, 54, 71, 79, 109, 110, 111, 112, 115, 129, n. 41, 130 nn. 3, 13, 132 nn. 47, 48, 49, 50, 65, 134 n. 31, 135 nn. 60, 61, 140 n. 10, 141 nn. 13, 16, 19, 23, 142 nn. 24, 25, 26, 28, 29

Rules of the college, 112–113, 116

Rum, 3, 45, 46, 54, 59, 65, 69–70, 72–73, 79

St. Andrew's parish, Barbados, 111

St. Asaph, Bishop of, 37. *See also* Drummond, Robert Hay

St. Augustine's, Canterbury, England, 121

St. Christopher, 16, 29, 66, 88

St. Dominque, 81

St. George's parish, Barbados, 140 n. 4

St. James's parish, Barbados, 111, 140 n. 4

St. John's parish, Barbados, 91, 111, 117

St. Joseph's parish, Barbados, 140 n. 4

St. Lucy's parish, Barbados, 111, 140 n. 4

St. Michael's parish, Barbados, 140 n. 4

St. Paul's grammar school, 108

St. Peter's All Saints parish, Barbados, 140 n. 4

St. Philip's parish, Barbados, 111, 140 n. 4

St. Thomas's parish, Barbados, 140 n. 4

St. Vincent's, 79

Say, Mr., joint manager of Codrington estates, 55

School, Codrington grammar: advanced instruction, 112, 118; books, 113, 120; closed, 37, 109, 117; curriculum, 113, 114, 118; discipline, 112–113, 116; early delays, 109; expansion, 118; experiment, 118; fees, 118; finances, 109, 115, 118; higher education, 118; initial organization, 111; instruction, 113; library, 113, 114; modeled on English schools, 112; opened, 35, 110, 117; operating costs, 116–117; personnel, 112; problems, 53; religious instruction, 113; repairs, 59; rules, 116; schedule, 113, 116, 118, 143–144 n. 58; sciences, 114; at close of eighteenth century, 117; supplies for, 113, 114; texts, 113, 120, 143–144 n. 58. *See also* Codrington College; Education; Grammar school; Schoolmasters; Students

Schoolbooks, 113

Schoolmasters of Codrington College and school: 141 n. 15; ability to train men, 115; as attorneys, 54, 55, 111, 115; backgrounds, 115; correspondence, 37; difficulties, 115; disputes with attorneys, 53–54; requirements for, 116; salary, 59;

Timber, scarcity of, 46. *See also* Codrington College, materials for

Town agent for Codrington estates, 50, 52, 72. *See also* Agent

Transportation, 59; costs, 73–74; problems, 54, 72, 76

Transshipment of sugar from Bridgetown, 73

Trattle, Marmaduke, 135 n. 46

Treadway, Nathan, teacher, 142 n. 33

Trinidad, 87

Utrecht, Peace of, 10, 11

Vaughton, John, nephew of John Smalridge and acting manager of estates, 34, 52–53

Walker, Alexander, sponsor of school, 29

Walker, Robert, 140 n. 97

Walker, William, of Barbados, 29

Walpole, Horace, 3, 133 n. 7

War, danger to shipment of sugar, 73, 75, 81

Warburton, William, 9

Water and sugar production, 63

Weather and sugar production, 62, 70, 75, 76

Weeks, Henry, tenant, 111

Weeks, Ralph, foundation student, 111

Wells, English theological college, 121

West Indian education, 18, 106, 121; society, 3, 93; world, 87. *See also* Barbadians; Barbados; Planters

West Indies, 62, 64, 86; competition, 3; master-slave relations, 85; sugar production, 81

Wharton, Thomas, catechist to Negroes, 90, 95, 97, 98, 136 n. 6, 138 n. 62, 139 n. 74

Wheler, Sir George, 19

White education, 86, 96, 97, 106, 117, 136 n. 6, 143 n. 51. *See also* Codrington College; Education; School

Wilkey, John, 111

Wilkey, William, foundation student, 111

Wilkie, Thomas, catechist to Negroes, 89, 91, 92, 137 nn. 24, 34, 35, 36

William and Mary, College of, 106

Williams, Reynolds, foundation student, 141 n. 21

Williams, Thomas, 141 n. 21

Williams, Thomas, sponsor of school for Antigua, 29

Willet, Ralph, sponsor of school for St. Christopher's, 29

Willis, Richard, 19

Wind and sugar production, 48, 49, 64, 68, 71

Windmills, 27, 65, 68

Windsor, Ontario, 121

Woodbridge, Dudley, attorney and sponsor of school, 23, 28, 29, 31, 125 n. 1, 126 n. 29, 127 nn. 30, 33, 34, 128 n. 18, 130 n. 1

Worsley, Henry, governor of Barbados, 51, 90, 109, 131 n. 36, 137 n. 31, 140 n. 5

Writing master, 117

Wyse, George Liddal, sponsor of school for St. Christopher's, 29

Yale College, 106

"Yambs," 79

Yam seeds, 76

Yellow fever epidemic, 80